# Praise for
## Spirituality in the Workplace:
### What it is
### Why it Matters
### How to Make it Work for You

"*Reading this book will help business executives and employees understand that spirituality in the workplace has nothing to do with religion, and everything to do with mutuality, acceptance, holistically embracing the totality of who we are as human beings so that we can bring that whole person to the workplace. The results to be achieved will lead to excellence in the performance of our duties on behalf of all stakeholders of the enterprise. This practical review of spirit at work and the tools the authors provide will definitely enhance the quality of life for you and for your co-workers, while stimulating a true peak-performance workplace to emerge.*"

**–Rinaldo Brutoco**
President, World Business Academy
President and CEO, ShangriLa Consulting, Inc.

"*This book offers another way, the way of spirituality in the workplace. This new paradigm is a natural evolution of earlier management theories and approaches, and Joan Marques, Satinder Dhiman, and Richard King are pioneers in this evolution.*"

**–Judi Neal**
Executive Director, Association for Spirit at Work

*"This is a very important book that ought to be read by every student and practitioner of management."*

**–Ian Mitroff**
Author, *A Spiritual Audit of Corporate America: A Hard Look at Spirituality, Religion, and Values in the Workplace*
J-B Warren Bennis Series

*"With the rapidly increasing trend toward globalization, understanding, meaning, and fulfillment—tools toward enhanced satisfaction and improved organizational performance—have become more important than ever. Whether you work in a business or non-profit environment, locally or globally,* Spirituality in the Workplace *is a book you need to read in order to stay focused in today's and tomorrow's world."*

**–Gary Hickman**
President, Junior Achievement of Southern California

Joan Marques
Satinder Dhiman
Richard King

# Spirituality in the Workplace:
# What it is
# Why it Matters
# How to Make it Work for You

Spirituality in the Workplace:
What it is
Why it Matters
How to Make it Work for You

Published by

PERSONHOOD PRESS
P.O. Box 370
Fawnskin, CA 92333
800-429-1192
personhoodpress@att.net
www.personhoodpress.com

ISBN: 1-932181-23-7
Library of Congress Control Number: 2007920743

Cover Design: Linda Jean Thille – Blackstone Arts
Editing: Dean Huffaker – Circadian Productions

Printed in the United States of America

This book is dedicated to all members of the global workforce who seek more meaning and connection at work.

May this work provide you new insights
that reinforce the spiritual perspectives
you already carry within.

# Contents

# Spirituality in the Workplace:
# What it is
# Why it Matters
# How to Make it Work for You

## Foreword

I am often asked if spirituality in the workplace is a movement, and my answer is, yes, it is. Individuals and corporate leaders show a steadily increasing interest in creating organizations that nurture the human spirit. Yet, walk into almost any corporation these days and you still find an organization full of fear, anger, resistance to change, and employees who are there just for the paycheck. The best employees are usually looking to go elsewhere, and the employees who are not so marketable are trying to stay under the radar and just hang on for dear life. Is this a formula for high productivity and high performance? Is this the way to create a sustainable organization? I think not.

This book offers another way, the way of spirituality in the workplace. This new paradigm is a natural evolution of earlier management theories and approaches, and Joan Marques, Satinder Dhiman, and Richard King are pioneers in this evolution. A very brief overview of the development of management thought over the past century can help provide some context.

The earliest management theories were developed by people in the early 20th century with an engineering approach, most notably Frederick Taylor. His focus was on the physical effectiveness and efficiency of workers. He saw the human body as an extension of the machine, and studied ways to utilize the human machine with as little wasted energy and motion as possible.

The next phase of management thought came out of the Hawthorne studies and similar work in the 1930s and 1940s. These studies actually originated as Tayloristic industrial engineering studies of the effects of lighting on worker efficiency. However, there was an anachronistic finding that led the researchers to conclude that emotional and social needs were just as important to high performance as physical efficiency.

In the late 1970s and throughout the 1990s, an expansion of management theories included focus not just on the workers as physical beings, or as emotional beings, but also as thinking beings. With the advent of quality circles and similar approaches came the recognition that workers did not check their minds at the door when they came to work, but, in fact, they were actually the experts at their jobs and probably knew more about how to make things better than the engineers.

As our concept of what it means to be human is expanding, so too are our management theories expanding. With recent research in quantum physics and holistic medicine, people are coming to accept that humans are also spiritual beings, that we are the sum of body, emotion, mind, and spirit. Pioneers such as the authors of this book have been teaching management theories and practices that now include our spiritual nature.

As crass as this may sound, spirituality is the new competitive edge. Most organizations are physically efficient, and they attend to the emotional and social needs of employees to some degree. They have learned how to involve employees in decision making and to tap their intellectual abilities. But how many have learned to tap into the human spirit?

When I talk about spirituality and human spirit, I mean two things: first, I mean a connection to something greater than ourselves, whatever you might call it; second, I mean a sense of meaning and purpose that guides our lives.

This book makes a strong business case as well as a moral case for the importance of spirituality in the workplace. It also provides you with practical steps and models that will help you to unleash that creative and passionate energy that comes from the Transcendent. Organizations that learn how to unleash this energy will be more innovative, will be able to use intuition to make effective decisions, will be able to attract and retain high-integrity and high-performing employees, and will make a positive difference in their communities and in the world.

Part of my own personal mission has been to identify organizations that are open about their commitment to spirituality in the workplace and to tell their stories. With the help of many wonderful people, we have created the International Spirit at Work Awards; as of 2006 we have identified and honored 36 organizations in eleven different countries. As you read this book, you may want to refer to the case studies of these organizations at www.spiritatwork.org.

I see these organizations as akin to Roger Bannister's four minute mile. Before Roger ran a mile in less than four minutes, the experts of the day believed that it was humanly impossible to run the mile faster than four minutes. It had never been done. But once Roger broke that barrier, several people were able to replicate his feat in the following year. Most people, when they hear the phrase *spirituality in the workplace*, say, "Isn't that an oxymoron?" They think that it is impossible to work in an organization with principles of love, kindness, humility, and compassion. Yet these 36 organizations prove that it is not only possible, it is good business.

It is my sincere hope that, as you read this book, you find the courage and inspiration to help your organization to live in alignment with deeper spiritual principles, and that you find creative ways to nurture the human spirit of all those who are touched by your organization. The world desperately needs a shift in consciousness in business, and every organization that takes steps in the direction of greater spirituality in the workplace is making a significant difference.

Judi Neal, Ph.D.
Executive Director
Association for Spirit at Work
East Haven, CT
September 2006

# Part I

## Spirituality in the Workplace: What it Is

### Definitions and History

# Chapter 1

# Meaning of Spirituality in the Workplace

*One day a man came across three stonecutters working in a quarry. Each one was cutting out a block of stone. Curious, he asked the first stonecutter what he was doing. "What? Are you blind?" the stonecutter shouted, "Can't you see, I'm cutting this stupid piece of stone." Shocked, but still no wiser, the man turned to the second stonecutter and asked him what he was doing. "I am cutting this block of stone to make sure that its sides are straight and smooth so that the builder can build a straight wall." Feeling a lot better, but still not really any wiser, the man turned to the third stonecutter, who seemed to be the happiest of the three, and asked him what he was doing. "I am building a cathedral," the third stonecutter replied.*

> This chapter will explain the confusion that lies at the root of business executives' possible aversion to refer to their workplace as a spiritual one. Since we are reviewing various study findings, as well as an extensive amount of literature in this book, we will start by presenting our assumptions here before engaging into definitions of the phenomenon. Spirituality in the workplace will then be reviewed as an emerging paradigm in the third part of this chapter, after which we will end with the presentation of various definitions and perceived crucial factors for a spiritual workplace.

### The Confusion

Although the term *spirituality in the workplace* has increasingly gained popularity in the past few years, there still seems to be much confusion around the topic. According to Judi Neal, this confusion occurs predominantly when managers confuse *spirituality* with *religion*.[1] Some authors believe that you can have a deepening of the spiritual experience at work without shoving a particular point of view down people's throats.[2] Others feel that the language of spirituality in the workplace is grounded in the traditions of religious imagery.[3]

> *The bond that links your true family is not one of blood, but of respect and joy in each other's life.*
> Richard Bach

From the foregoing, it is apparent that confusion exists regarding the meaning of the terms *spirituality* and *religion;* the term *spirituality* clearly means various things to various people.(4) You may find one author who explains that spirituality at work is "something we all possess,"(5) while another refers to spirituality in the context of employees who understand themselves as spiritual beings whose souls need nourishment at work, and who wish to experience a sense of purpose and meaning in their work and a sense of connectedness to one another and to their workplace community.(6) While none of these explanations is wrong, they demonstrate a wide divergence of opinions as to what spirituality at work really means.

Accordingly, one of our main purposes in studying spirituality at work was to establish a more general perspective on the topic by formulating a broadly acceptable definition of spirituality in the workplace, and then to identify the essential elements of a spiritual workplace. Our initial study focused on business executives, but as we continued to gain information and insights in the ensuing years, we expanded our findings based on the views of middle, lower, and non-managerial workers in addition to executives.

## Assumptions

To ensure consistency in understanding the topic, we start by outlining the assumptions we went on throughout our studies. Although these assumptions may seem minimal to some and redundant to others, they have served to establish a clear perspective for the research:

1. The first assumption is that spirituality exists in the workplace. An abundance of material proves that authors, leaders, and members of the general workforce at various levels increasingly recognize and discuss this trend. Based on the widespread availability of material on the subject, we see no need to prove the existence of spirit at work, as we take it to be an established fact.

2. The second assumption is the existence of both elements included in the concept of *spirituality in the workplace*:

a. Spirituality has been an intriguing topic throughout human existence. As indicated above, spirituality means many different things to many different people.(7) The enormous body of literature on the topic of spirituality, of which we will review a small selection later in this chapter, serves as evidence of the broad interest and variety in experience existing around it. Because there is so much material already available on the topic, the scope of our study precludes an in-depth explanation of the broader topic of spirituality.

> *The foundations of a person are not in matter but in spirit.*
> Ralph Waldo Emerson

b. We define the *workplace* as a meeting place of the people employed by an organization. The variety of workplaces has only expanded in past decades, from a growing number of possible physical locations to an even greater number of virtual ones. For this reason, we can accept workplaces as a generally established fact.

3. The third assumption is that every person has spirituality; therefore, every *working* person has spirituality as well. Thus, in this book we look at spirituality as an environmental factor that can be present in all possible work settings. We have therefore set no limitations to the fields of the people we reviewed in our research. In other words, spirituality can be applied and experienced in any and every type of workplace.

These three assumptions served as the foundation of our research of spirituality in the workplace.

## An Emerging Paradigm

> *Work is a spiritual journey for many of us, although we talk about it in different ways.*

The emerging paradigm we call "spirituality in the workplace" is expressed in many ways: Some authors say that a fundamental tension between rational goals and spiritual fulfillment now haunts workplaces around the world, and that survey after management survey affirms that a majority want to find meaning in their work.(8) Other authors hold that something has been stirring in workers' souls for quite some time now—a longing for deeper meaning, deeper connection, greater simplicity, a connection to something higher.(9) Bruce Jentner, president of Jentner Financial Group in Bath, Ohio, recognizes this trend: "I have a deep conviction that everybody has a need for something bigger in life than just making money and going to work."(10) Other authors view the topic even more broadly, describing work as a spiritual journey for many of us, although we talk about it in different ways.(11)

It seems that there is an overall agreement among researchers that a major transformation is occurring in today's organizations.(12) To underscore the point, a survey conducted a few years ago by human resource strategists Act-1 found that 55 percent of the 1,000 workers polled consider spirituality to play a significant role in the workplace. In addition, a third of those cited (34 percent) said that the role had increased since the September 11, 2001 terrorist acts.(13)

A 1999 issue of *U.S. News & World Report* revealed that, in the preceding decade, more than 300 titles on workplace spirituality—from Jesus CEO to The Tao of Leadership—had flooded the bookstores. Indeed, 30 MBA programs now offer courses on the issue. A recent issue of the *Harvard School Bulletin* focused on the trend as well. Signs of this sudden concern for corporate soul are showing up everywhere, from boardrooms to company lunchrooms, from business conferences to management newsletters, from management consulting firms to business schools. Echoing Andre Malraux, who said that this new century's task will be to rediscover its gods—some management thinkers are prophesying that the effective leaders of this century will be spiritual leaders.(14)

Organizations increasingly realize how shortsighted it is to focus solely on financial success at the expense of humanistic values. Since the beginning of the new millennium, a growing number of organizations have tried to discover ways to help employees balance work and family, and to create conditions wherein each person can realize his or her potential while fulfilling the requirements of the job. One writer has called such enlightened organizations "incubators of the spirit."

> *The effective leaders of 21st century will be spiritual leaders.*

Work has ceased to be just a "nine-to-five thing," and is increasingly seen as an important element in fulfilling one's destiny. As James Autry observed, "Work can provide the opportunity for spiritual and personal, as well as financial, growth. If it doesn't, we are wasting far too much of our lives on it." Leading others is now seen as an extension of managing ourselves. The implications of this change are clear: On one hand, it is about working collectively, reflectively, and spiritually smarter; on the other hand, it implies employment that is mind-enriching, heart-fulfilling, and soul-satisfying, as well as financially rewarding.

Many individuals, including business executives, management theorists, researchers, and employees in general, confirm the emergence of this organizational transformation.(15) These sources generally conclude that American society and its political and legal institutions are moving toward a more open, value-expressive environment that will put even greater pressure on companies to honor employees' requests for spiritual accommodation. One author pointed out a dramatic upsurge in interest in spirituality even among those who study, teach, and write about business management.(16) This new interest is also apparent among practicing managers.

## Defining Spirituality

*Webster's* defines spirituality as relating to, consisting of, or affecting the spirit; relating to sacred matters; concerned with religious values; of, related to, or joint in spirit. The term *spirituality* comes from the Latin *spiritus*, which means vapor, breath, air or wind.

> *Spirituality is the desire to find ultimate purpose in life, and to live accordingly.*

Gerald Cavanagh provided an interesting illustration of the divergence of opinions regarding the definition of spirituality. He cited Ian Mitroff, professor of management and author on this topic, who defined spirituality as "the desire to find ultimate purpose in life, and to live accordingly." Cavanagh compared Mitroff's definition to others that define spirituality "loosely as energy, meaning, knowing, etc." Reviewing authors who relied heavily on Taoist, Buddhist, Hindu, Zen, and Native American spiritualities, Cavanagh saw these non-Western perspectives as superior in integrating personal life, work, leisure, prayer, religion, and other aspects of life.(17)

Willa Marie Bruce enumerated opinions on spirituality in a 2000 edition of *The American Review of Public Administration*:

> Only modest agreement on the definition of spirituality exists. For one Catholic theologian, spirituality is "the way we orient ourselves toward the divine." For a physician at the Harvard Medical School, it is "that which gives meaning to life." For one social worker, it is "an individual search for meaning, purpose and values which may or may not include the concept of a God or transcendent being." For others, to be "Spiritual" means to know, and to live according to the knowledge, that there is more

9

to life than meets the eye. To be "spiritual" means, beyond that, to know, and to live according to the knowledge that God is present in us in grace as the principle of personal, interpersonal, social, and even cosmic transformation.(18)

Ian Mitroff and Elizabeth Denton, authors of *A Spiritual Audit of Corporate America*, explained their view on spirituality as informal and personal, that is, pertaining mainly to individuals. They also view spirituality as universal, non-denominational, broadly inclusive, and tolerant, and as the basic feeling of being connected with one's complete self, others, and the entire universe.(19)

Broadly speaking, spirituality encompasses the ultimate ends of life— the questions of meaning and purpose of life. The underlying assumption is that everyone and everything has a purpose. Spirituality assumes that there is more to life than our material self and existence. As one writer puts it, "We are not human beings on a spiritual journey; we are spiritual beings on a human journey." At its very best, it is our link to the deepest, most profound core of our existence. As Mitroff and Denton put it: "If a single word best captures the meaning of spirituality and the vital role it plays in people's lives, that word is interconnectedness."

Viewing life from a spiritual perspective provides a certain humility, a compelling sense of modesty about our existence and our place in the universe.

### Spirituality vs. Religion

Spirituality is distinct from institutionalized religion. While religion often directs people outward toward social rites and rituals, spirituality directs one inward toward the wealth of knowledge, senses, aspirations, and feelings one harbors within. Spirituality recognizes that there is something sacred at the core of all existence. Whatever its source, this one sacred element dwells within every living organism. Spirituality is a non-dogmatic, non-exclusive, non-patriarchal, and gender-neutral approach to connect with this one source of all existence. Regardless of our outward differences, there is an underlying sacred commonality, *the ground of being*, to borrow a phrase from Paul Tillich. The essence of this difference and commonality is displayed in the title of Mortimer Adler's book, *Truth in Religion: Plurality of Religions and Unity of Truth*.(20)

## Spirituality in the Workplace: The Many Definitions

The fact that there are so many different views of spirituality in the workplace is one of the issues that makes this phenomenon so intriguing. Brenda Freshman, author of a study that analyzed definitions and applications of spirituality in the workplace, made a few interesting observations in this regard:

1.  Not any one, two, or even three things can be said about spirituality in the workplace that would include the universe of explanations.

> *Defining spirituality in the workplace is like capturing an angel. Explaining spirituality at work is ethereal and beautiful, but perplexing.*

2.  There is no one answer to the question, "What is spirituality in the workplace?"

3.  Definitions and applications of spirituality in the workplace are unique to individuals. One must be careful not to presuppose otherwise. Therefore, when planning any group or organizational intervention around the topic, the suggestion is made to derive definitions and goals from the participants themselves.

4.  [There are] many possible ways to understand such a complex and diverse area as spirituality in the workplace.(21)

Freshman's findings demonstrated once again the complexity and multiple interpretability of this topic. Yet another author, Jennifer Laabs, seemed to agree with all of the above when she pointed out that defining spirituality in the workplace is like capturing an angel. Laabs felt that explaining spirituality at work is ethereal and beautiful, but perplexing.(22) And so, it surfaces once again: the term *spirituality* means many things to many people.

> *Spirituality in the workplace is an experience of interconnectedness among those involved in a work process.*

After in-depth study of the topic, Giacalone and Jurkiewicz defined a spiritual workplace as a "framework of organizational values evidenced in the culture that promote employees' experience of transcendence through the work process, facilitating their sense of being connected to others in a way that provides feelings of completeness and joy."(23)

Based on the findings of our phenomenological study in 2003, and following some modification through subsequent research, we have formulated the following definition of spirituality in the workplace:

> *Spirituality in the workplace is an experience of interconnectedness among those involved in a work process, initiated by authenticity, reciprocity, and personal goodwill; engendered by a deep sense of meaning that is inherent in the organization's work; and resulting in greater motivation and organizational excellence.*

After conducting additional research among business executives in 2004 and 2005, we compiled a list of phrases that exemplify spirituality in the workplace:

- Vision as a concentration on the greater good, passion, and purpose;
- Enhancement of personal fulfillment and creativity through spirituality and enlightenment;
- Work as a life-fulfilling activity—not as a means to simply fund an otherwise personally fulfilling life;
- Work as a contribution toward an integrated life;
- Seeing the potential for businesses to achieve enhanced goals by helping their people at all levels achieve personal fulfillment through their work.

The 2003 definition, in addition to the 2004/2005 characterizations presented above, serve as the development interpretation for the subsequent chapters of this book.

## Reflection Sheet

These areas represent the contents of this chapter that I consider applicable to my life:

These areas represent the contents of this chapter whose applicability to my life I question:

My personal opinions after reading this chapter:

What I would like to remember:

# Chapter 2

# Need for a
# Spiritual
# Workplace

In this chapter we will present a number of pressing matters that have prompted the increasing call for spirituality in the workplace. We will particularly review some of the mentality issues in the average U.S. corporate workplace that we identify as potential obstacles toward the establishment of this affirmative mindset in work environments.

## Reasons for the Call for a Spiritual Workplace

*Organizations, which have long been viewed as rational systems, are considering making room for the spiritual dimension, a dimension that has less to do with rules and order and more with meaning, purpose, and a sense of community.*

 he current need for transformation in the workplace finds its foundation in a multitude of causes. Neal, for instance, thinks that the past few years—with 9/11, the market crash, the fall of Enron, and the lack of integrity in organizations—have caused people to hunger for more human connection and a deeper sense of meaning at work.(24)

Yet, the awareness of spirituality in the workplace was awakened long before the shocking terrorist acts of September 11, 2001. By 2000, Donde Ashmos and Dennis Duchon had already introduced the term *spirituality movement*, whereby they noted that organizations, which have long been viewed as rational systems, are considering making room for the spiritual dimension, a dimension that has less to do with rules and order and more to do with meaning, purpose, and a sense of community. Ashmos and Duchon subsequently listed five reasons for corporate America's growing interest in spirituality at work:

1. The downsizing, reengineering, and layoffs of the past decade, which have turned the American workplace into an environment where employees are demoralized;

2. The fact that the workplace is increasingly seen as a primary source of community for many people because of the decline of neighborhoods, churches, civic groups, and extended families as principal places for feeling connected;

3. The increased access to and enhanced curiosity about Pacific Rim cultures and Eastern philosophies. Philosophies such as Zen

Buddhism, Taoism, and Sufism encourage meditation and emphasize values such as group loyalty and finding one's spiritual center in every activity;

4. The fact that aging baby boomers are moving ever closer to life's greatest uncertainty—death—and thereby develop a growing interest in contemplating life's meaning;

5. The fact that there is increasing pressure of global competition, which has led organizational leaders to realize that employee creativity needs nurturing.(25)

Nonetheless, the above list is not exhaustive; other social scientists have added reasons to this enumeration, some of which are:

> *With the increased exposure to other ways of living, members of the entire global workforce are realizing the essence of balance in life: refraining from parking your values at the door of your workplace, thus bringing your entire self into work…*

- The arrival of the new millennium, which has made many people come to the realization that life progresses, and that at this monumental stage in time it might be suitable to rethink our behaviors toward one another if we want to continue the human race successfully;

- The increasing search for meaning through work, which is specifically fueled by the increasing numbers of higher education courses offered such as organizational behavior, spirituality in the workplace, workplace diversity, human resource management, leadership theory and practice, and courses that focus on doing international business. Through these courses, new members of the workforce become influenced to search for the meaning they are being taught in educational institutions, and to apply this mindset systematically wherever they work;

- The quest for stability in an unstable world, which ends up being a continuous quest, as change increases. Yet, employees want to feel comforted in an environment that is subject to multiple disruptions, triggered by constantly emerging global trends. The workplace, and therefore the team of colleagues at work, becomes a place where people seek support, trust, understanding, and all those other qualities that contribute to an emotionally stable environment;

- The movement towards more holistic living. With the increased exposure to other ways of living, other cultures, and other mindsets, and encouraged by the Internet, members of the entire global workforce are realizing the essence of balance in life; refraining from parking your values at the door of your workplace, thus bringing your entire self into work, and spending quality time with loved ones are some of the outgrowths of the movement toward more holistic living;

- The greater influx of women in the workplace. Women are known for their nurturing and non-confrontational ways of solving problems, while still keeping track of the goals that need to be reached. With the percentage of women increasing in the workplace, styles of decision making and entire work processes are being reexamined;

- Developed countries' progression from belly needs to brain needs. The so-called industrialized countries are evolving their economies toward service orientation and brain product output rather than manufacturing output. This change instigates a trend of rethinking values and connections. Increasingly, brainworkers on one continent team up with brainworkers on other continents as well as manufacturing units on yet other continents. This brings about a greater sense of interconnectedness, which, in turn, instigates increased realization of the need for spirit at work.

### The Paradox of Contemporary Workplace Mentality

> *Competition could become a significant threat toward a cooperative mindset if it is encouraged too forcefully among colleagues.*

One problem that many thinkers on the topic of spirituality in the workplace seem to overlook is the current workplace mentality in the United States, which supports individualism and competition in every area of the work environment. Although competition may be considered a driving factor among various business organizations in any industry, when it is encouraged too forcefully among colleagues it could become a significant threat to the cooperative mindset that spirituality in the workplace advocates.

Various management books promote the mindset of conflict in the workplace, explaining that constructive conflict can lead to the development of new, improved, and more efficient work methods, while destructive conflict puts the work relationships and productivity in a downward spiral.

Although there is some truth to this philosophy, it leaves little room for the perspective of cooperation, in which co-workers develop and maintain such a high level of understanding and work motivation that they assist each other without inhibitions, and solve problems that surface in the workplace at a much higher rate. In encouraging the conflict and competition perspective, management theorists often neglect the fact that constant striving can lead to fast but mediocre and short-lived results, and can prevent co-workers from cohering effectively enough to examine the bigger picture of their performance in order to establish a structurally better running department.

Another current attitudinal workplace problem is that of changed inter-human approaches that we have witnessed in the past decades throughout work environments in this country. The older generation of readers may remember "the good old days" in U.S. workplaces when people got holiday turkeys or gift baskets instead of gift certificates, and when there were regular boat trips or picnics for families.

> *It may very well be that the escalating number of lawsuits in recent years lies at the core of the present cautious and impersonal approach of many U.S. corporations.*

These older readers may also recall the liveliness that preceded those events: the female colleagues agreeing among themselves on the dishes to prepare, and the male employees making well-coordinated plans. The essence of these gatherings was to bring employees of all levels together and give them the opportunity to get to know each other in a different setting. It increased the mutual bond, and it enhanced understanding and empathy.

However, somewhere down the line the majority of U.S. companies decided that a present around the holidays was just too much hassle, and that the risk of organizing family days was too great. Employees or their family members could get hurt during the event, and the company could easily be sued over a serious or a frivolous issue. In other words, a seemingly innocent gathering could become hazardous for the corporation and its very existence!

Here is a point to ponder for all of us who favor the spirituality-at-work mindset: it is highly likely that the escalating number of lawsuits in recent years, even for harmless incidents, lies at the core of the present cautious and impersonal approach of many U.S. corporations. Understandable yet unfortunate, for, at the same time, the sense of togetherness and acceptance toward one another, and seeing each other as more than just a production factor in the work setting, has diminished accordingly.

The above-described trend reveals a paradox in regard to the surging call for spirituality at work. Increasingly, authors, workplace analysts, social researchers, and maturing employees call for better understanding between co-workers at all levels in the belief that it will enhance the willingness among employees to contribute more than just the required skills and give people who spend so many hours with each other a better sense of purpose and a higher level of satisfaction. The key word here is *interconnectedness*; however, interconnectedness will remain a utopian ideal if people are denied the one activity that would enhance it in the first place—getting to know and value each other as whole beings. For this process, gatherings outside the workplace play an important role.

We may as well admit it: indirectly, this estrangement from family activities has been caused by the same society that now yearns for it. In other words, the current absence of spirituality in the workplace may have been brought upon us by ourselves.

It is, after all, unattractive for any organization to continue sponsoring extra-work activities if the risk of a multimillion-dollar lawsuit lurks behind every employee or family member's mishap. The business environment is a hard one and competitive enough as it is. Business organizations have to remain on their toes in order to stay abreast of the developments in their area of expertise. New inventions, and the subsequent changes in market demands, occur at a much faster pace than ever.

> The current absence of spirituality in the workplace may have been brought upon us by ourselves.

Spirituality in the workplace can be an invaluable contribution toward better relationships in the work environment, raising productivity through increased cooperation (as we will discuss below). However, it is often under-emphasized by employers, not necessarily by choice but as a result of the ever present threat of escalating and costly repercussions of an overly litigious society.

## Insights Obtained from the Increased Call for
## Spirituality in the Workplace

In the following section we will discuss three main insights gained from the increased call for spirituality in the workplace. Then, we will elaborate on some of the major advantages of applying this mindset versus some major disadvantages of not doing so. We will subsequently examine one of the main reasons that today's corporate workplaces remain unspiritual.

*Spirituality in the workplace* is a term that, for some, merely means yet a new buzzword in the business environment. Fortunately for an increasing number of business executives and employees at various levels, the concept is emerging into a serious trend that can no longer be brushed aside with an annoyed shrug or rejected with the reproof that it is just another disguise for instilling religion into work environments. Up to this point we have provided a number of reasons for taking this trend seriously. After reviewing all statements made in our research and comparing them to the existing literature on the topic, we have identified three main insights in the minds of members of corporate America:

1.  The first and least complicated insight we have distinguished in the American workforce is the realization that something is wrong with the majority of our work environments. More and more people want to feel comfortable and important in their workplace. They do not want to be considered yet another name tag with yet another set of functions to fulfill. Employees want to be recognized for who they are—people, with families, ups and downs, skills and talents, and diverging yet oftentimes very useful perspectives.

    > *Treat people as if they were what they ought to be and you help them to become what they are capable of being.*
    >
    > Johann Wolfgang von Goethe

2.  The second and slightly more comprehensive realization is that the implementation of spirituality in the workplace is not happening as smoothly and rapidly as some may have expected. This unfortunate setback has a number of important reasons of a persistent nature at the core including cultural values and social trends that have been in place for almost a century and are therefore very hard to correct. The individualistic mindset of the average U.S. corporate worker and its encouragement from childhood on immediately come to mind. While spirituality in the workplace calls for an interconnected approach and an enhanced level of trust among

employees at various levels, the bare-bones reality is that we learn not to trust anyone but ourselves—definitely in the workplace, where we learn "everyone may be after your position."

3.  The third realization, although more subtle in nature, may be the hardest to overcome on our way toward comprehensive implementation of spirituality in the workplace. It pertains to the human tendency to surround ourselves with similar-looking and like-minded associates, because this guarantees faster decision making, less time investment in learning about each others' perspectives, and a higher level of reflectivity. In other words, the human inclination tends toward homogeneity rather than diversity. The implementation of diversity has brought with it much upheaval, which can now consequentially be traced as a particular point of attention on practically all corporate Web sites. Unfortunately, the comfort zone of remaining surrounded by kindred individuals, predominantly based on backgrounds and looks rather than on mindsets, has turned out to be more persistent than many could initially estimate.

## Need for a More Spiritual Workplace

In a review of workplace trends since the 40s and 50s, which ran from company picnics and anti-smoking programs to on-site yoga sessions, Raizel Robin concluded that people now "have made the link between mental health, productivity and absenteeism—and the whole notion that people who are happy at home and happy at work are more productive in the workplace." However, Robin also found that the well-being of knowledge workers is suffering. She categorized modern knowledge workers (not to be confused with Peter Drucker's information technology workers) as all those who put their college degree to work in any work environment. Robin claimed that work for these employees can be physically strenuous, contributing to illnesses such as heart disease and diabetes, and nervous disorders like anxiety and depression. Calling for wellness initiatives in the workplace, Robin advised business corporations to particularly ensure that such initiatives are implemented regularly. While wellness programs are the first to be discontinued in tight budget times, Robin warned, "a worn-out, unhealthy workforce is a costly one." She also stated that, even in workplaces that offer wellness programs and employee facilitation projects, top management often maintains a culture that seems to discourage employees from making proper use of the accommodators.(26) Indeed, how many of us have not faced the stress

> *People who are happy at home and happy at work are more productive in the workplace.*
> Raizel Robin

of wanting to spend more time with our loved ones versus meeting the deadline for an immense project at work?

## Disadvantages of Failing to Implement Spirit at Work

Alert authors warn that, despite an extensive set of critiques and criticisms offered by scholars and practitioners, most modern organizations lack a spiritual foundation and deny their employees the opportunity of spiritual expression through their work.(27) The neglect and ignorance that corporations exhibit bring about higher costs and damages than they are willing to acknowledge.

The most obvious costs result from hiring and training new entrants to the workplace at a higher pace due to high turnover rates. The high level of absenteeism that is also part of the culture in these work environments is another factor to consider: because people endure higher levels of stress and resentment in these unpleasant, high-pressure workplaces, they use every opportunity to stay away. Worse, their resentment toward having to perform in such an environment creates various psychosomatic symptoms within them, providing them with genuine reasons to stay home.

> *Top management often maintains a culture that seems to discourage workers from making use of wellness programs.*
> Raizel Robin

The increasing numbers of absentees place excessive pressure on the employees who show up, so that they, in turn, get overworked and become discontent about their workplace; thus, the downward spiral is established. One should not underestimate the level of aggravation that emerges among employees who continuously have to fill in for colleagues who are absent. This regular trend of double-working for the same pay finally motivates these employees to look for another job.

## Advantages of Applying Spirit at Work

The authors cited above also referred to the potential benefits to managers, employees, and society of a spiritually oriented workplace. It follows logically that employees who feel connected and find meaning in their workplace perform better, show up more often, and contribute more proactively to a better atmosphere in the workplace.

A team of researchers presented four interesting advantages in their review of employees who maintain the spiritual mindset:

1.  The stronger the spiritual factor of personality, the more tolerant the person is of work failure, and the less susceptible the person is to stress.
2.  The stronger the spiritual factor of personality, the more the person favors the democratic style of leadership, the more trusting the person is, and the higher the person's tolerance is of human diversity.
3.  The stronger the spiritual factor of personality, the more the person exhibits altruistic behavior and citizenship.
4.  The stronger the spiritual factor of personality, the more the person's commitment to the organization and work group increases.(28)

Yet another major advantage of nurturing the spiritual mindset within each employee in the organization is that of ethicality. A team of authors on this issue found, "Fundamental aspects of workplace spirituality such as meaningful work that provides a feeling of purpose, a sense of connection and positive social relations with co-workers, and the ability to live an integrated life in which the work role does not conflict with the essential nature of person as a human being, may interact to create different perceptions of ethicality within the organization."(29)

> The stronger the spiritual factor of personality, the more tolerant the person is of work failure, and the less susceptible the person is to stress.
> Mohamed et al

The statement made above has merit; one would indeed assume that an employee with an elevated spiritual approach toward life would be more attuned into doing the right things for the right reasons, even though the actions may vary from person to person. These authors therefore conclude that the "degree of individual spirituality influences whether an individual perceives a questionable business practice as ethical or unethical." They maintain that the "predominance of personal ethical standards applied to organizational environments is driven by employees' growing desire to merge their personal and professional values, viewing their career as an avenue through which to express themselves and make a positive difference in the world." The authors further feel that this is particularly true of today's emerging workforce, explaining the reasons as follows: "While employees are generally insecure and frightened at work, they increasingly depend upon [work] environments for primary links to other people as more traditional support systems have weakened."(30)

25

Author Debbie Carter, underscored this perspective in stating that "the ethics or morals of our organizations are becoming increasingly important to employees."(31) Carter cited an article by Chris Sangster, who wrote, "Spirituality can be seen basically as displaying and applying a heightening level of awareness towards others in a selfless way. The benefits of such an approach are clearly greater staff loyalty and retention leading to increased creativity and productivity." Sangster reemphasized an often-presented clarification in context of spirituality in the workplace when he placed religion out of the scope, stressing that "it is possible to lead a 'spiritual' way of life without following any particular religious path." In Sangster's opinion, spiritual workers are those who

> *Spirituality can be seen as displaying and applying a heightening level of awareness toward others in a selfless way.*
> Chris Sangster

> think co-operatively and/or altruistically; have a balanced, objective view of the world; listen as much as (or more than) they speak; apply three-dimensional bigger picture thinking; believe in some higher driving force and purpose beyond humankind; find the time to think things through objectively; think laterally in order to promote realistic solutions; encourage and empower others selflessly; work open-mindedly with a wide range of people; consistently display integrity and trust, and; expect the best from people without being a "soft touch."

Like many other authors, Sangster acknowledges the fact that spirituality in the workplace, as a term, is perceived somewhat cautiously and suspiciously by business corporate leaders; he therefore recommends the term *holistic thinking* as typical of the mindset of a spiritual worker. He subsequently asserts that "one of the key principles for applying holistic thinking successfully within business is the simple concept of the three-step continuum: belonging, assertion, and cooperation." In foundation, Sangster explains that a spiritual worker will first elevate him- or herself toward increased confidence, after which he or she will assist others in achieving this level of performance as well through mentorism. Hence, the upward spiral is established. Sangster offers a final warning to corporations: "In order for this level of motivation to be maintained, it is crucial that these individuals get the required ongoing support from both superiors and the company itself."(32) In line with Sangster's statements, Gul and Doh "advance the position that for spirit in the workplace to be fully realized, organizations must enable the unfolding of each individual though his or her participation in the work of the organization."(33)

## Why Today's Corporate Workplaces Remain Unspiritual

In an article published in *Training* in 2004, Heather Johnson asserted that an incredible 61 percent of adults believe their workplace would benefit from having a greater sense of spirituality, according to a recent survey conducted by Spirituality.com. Johnson referred to the exploding sales figures for self-help books of all sorts—an obvious sign that people are looking for guidance on how to live happier, more fulfilling lives. In her article, Johnson portrays the story of a man who, after 17 years, found that nothing in his life was functioning well: neither work, nor marriage, nor anything else. He finally decided to start writing, and although his book mentioned God as his CEO, this man, who is now a consultant and motivational speaker, explains that the essence of his book is about finding meaning. "It's not about forcing a religion. It's about offering a menu of things to think about that allows the worker to ultimately make a choice," writes Johnson, citing this turnaround person. She continues her citation, "You need to let who you are speak to what you believe. It doesn't come down to words and practices. It's taking what you believe and making decisions on what you believe."(34)

> *What is work and what is not work are questions that perplex the wisest of men.*
>
> Bhagavad Gita

Cases like the one described above are numerous in our society. After working for several years in an unspiritual work environment, many people find themselves searching for meaning. Those with entrepreneurial skills ultimately leap into a small venture in which they no longer have to endure the typical corporate, suffocating phenomenon of "little kingdoms, protected by little people." For, what is this whole trend about? Perhaps the entire foundation of unspiritual workplaces lies in the vulnerability that human beings detect within themselves, which they want to conceal at any price. In their fear of being overthrown by others who seem stronger or better equipped in certain ways; who seem to be descended from an unfamiliar culture, ethnicity, generation, or any other unfamiliar background or conviction; the fear mongers use all kinds of trivial ways to keep these perceived invaders out of the door, thereby protecting their position as if it were their life. The logical consequence of this hidden but very human vulnerability is that these people make life unbearable for others who enter the workplace with the best intentions, causing the new entrants to either bow to their invisible but very vividly sensed authority, or exit.

Agreed, it is hard to see the weakness under the steadfast shell of some authoritative people, but once discovered, it becomes easier to understand why so many workplaces are still unspiritual. It is the foundation of personal protectionism and the deeply ingrained fear of insecurity that causes those in leadership positions of so many work environments to seek and find their mental and emotional shelter in grudge, coercion, ridicule, harshness, backstabbing, setting up for failure, or hiding behind the misuse of phenomena such as jingoism, partisanship, and loyalty toward locals.

And these are exactly the demeanors that label a workplace as unspiritual, that form the basis of the cry of those who simply seek connection and work satisfaction for increased spirituality.

Based on the assertions made in this part of the chapter, Figure 2.1 on the next page clarifies the reasons that too many organizations are still unspiritual; the advantages of applying spirit at work; and the disadvantages of refraining from doing so. The figure portrays the descending trend of organizations that submit to the "traditional" mentalities of "-isms," while it also displays the ascending trend of institutions that practice the "-ties" that bind. The ultimate results of both trends also display the leadership style practiced in these two types of organizations: while the traditional trend ends in top-down leadership, the non-traditional trend results in bottom-up (servant-oriented) leadership.

## A Positive Endnote

On a more positive note, it seems that mid- and senior-level managers, according to a study conducted by Hanna Ashar and Maureen Lane-Maher, do not define success in materialistic terms—money, positional power, and status symbols—but instead use terms such as connection, balance, and wholeness to define and describe success. Even more encouraging, the participants in Ashar and Lane-Maher's study linked the concept of success to spirituality and stated that to be successful one needs to embrace spirituality as well.(35)

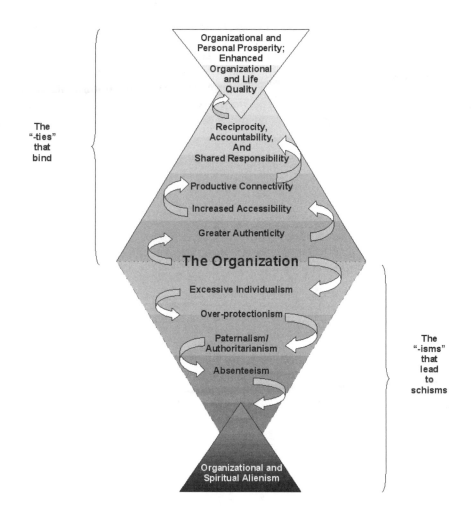

Figure 2.1. Why too many organizations lack a spiritual perspective.

It cannot be just a hollow desire when we state that spirituality in the workplace is on the rise, in spite of some of the setbacks mentioned in this chapter. It may even be constructive that the establishment of this mindset is encountering all the significant setbacks at one time, so that they can be dealt with acutely and eliminated effectively before a massive establishment of this phenomenon becomes fact. The number of employees that yearn for the application of spirituality in the workplace grossly exceeds the number of those who oppose it. If we have learned anything from the majority of Eastern cultures, it is that power resides in numbers. What more hopeful sign could there be?

*The only way to achieve true success is to express yourself completely in service to society.*

Aristotle

## Reflection Sheet

These areas represent the contents of this chapter that I consider applicable to my life:

_____
_____
_____
_____
_____
_____
_____
_____

These areas represent the contents of this chapter whose applicability to my life I question:

_____
_____
_____
_____
_____
_____
_____
_____
_____
_____

My personal opinions after reading this chapter:

_____
_____
_____
_____
_____
_____

What I would like to remember:

_____
_____
_____
_____
_____
_____
_____

# Chapter 3

# Fundamentals
# of a
# Spiritual
# Workplace

In this chapter we will review the factors that we consider necessary for a spiritual workplace and those that should be absent. To provide a better overview of these factors, we will divide them into three subcategories. Since the findings were gleaned from studies performed over a time span of three years, the factors will be presented in tables, so that the reader can get a better idea about the focus points in these studies. The factors will then be briefly discussed to emphasize proper interpretation.

## What is Necessary for a Spiritual Workplace?

> What work I have done I have done because it has been play. If it had been work I shouldn't have done it.
>
> Mark Twain

To address this question, we conducted in-depth research among business executives at various levels in a multitude of workplaces in Los Angeles. The main requirement for our interviews was that these individuals had to have done some deep thinking and reflection on spirituality in the workplace.

During analysis, we found that the entire list of words/phrases we gathered could be categorized under three main groups:

1. Internal factors;
2. Integrated factors;
3. External factors.

For a clear overview of all elements that were considered important in a spiritual workplace, we captured all factors in one table, dividing the factors across internal, integrated, and external spectrums. Guided by the fact that most of the people we interviewed clearly distinguished leadership responsibilities from actions performed by all employees who operate at a high level of spiritual awareness, we further divided the internal factors in two sub-categories: "Leadership," and "All Workers" (see Table 3.1 on next page).

In more detail, here are the essentials for a spiritual workplace:

- External elements include an appealing aesthetic atmosphere (plants, memorabilia, books), order, and the display of inspirational quotes.

Table 3.1. What is necessary for a spiritual workplace?

| External factors (Environment) | Integrated factors (Environment/ people) | Internal factors | |
|---|---|---|---|
| | | Leadership | All workers |
| • Aesthetic environment<br>• Order<br>• Motivational affirmations | • Peace<br>• Comfort<br>• Pleasant representation<br>• Accessibility of information<br>• Casualness (lack of protocol)<br>• Clubs and organizational functions<br>• Fair compensation and good reward mechanisms<br>• Charity from the organization to the community | • Sensitive, kind top executives<br>• Access to different levels of the organization | • Kind people<br>• Interaction<br>• Team performance<br>• Involvement<br>• More bonding of people, through commonality in character<br>• Reflection of leader's spiritual intent in the workplace<br>• Helping one another<br>• Prioritizing collective over personal goals<br>• Trust<br>• Respect<br>• Valuing differences<br>• Focus on solutions instead of problems<br>• Mentors<br>• A sense of mission that goes beyond the bottom line<br>• Conviviality among employees |

- Integrated elements include peace, comfort, a generally pleasant representation, accessibility of information, a certain level of casualness (lack of protocol), the existence of pleasant organizational subcultures such as clubs and organizational functions, fair compensation and good reward mechanisms, and the organization's involvement in charity projects in the community.

- Internal elements include:
  - Leadership Perspective: Top executives who are more sensitive, kind, and aware of the humane factor, which is reflected in their creation of a caring environment and accessibility to different levels of the organization;
  - All Workers' Perspective (leaders and employees): The reflection of the leaders' spiritual intent in the workplace such as the presence of kind people, high levels of interaction, team performance, involvement (meetings, encouraging mental contributions), and conviviality among employees. It also denotes the presence of an increased bonding among all workers through commonality in character traits, which manifests itself in high ethical and moral standards, as well as a culture of "givers" rather than "takers"; a tradition of helping one another; an attitude of prioritizing collective over personal goals; trust, respect, and valuing differences; a focus on solutions instead of problems; the presence of mentors; and a sense of mission that goes beyond the bottom line.

> *The only way to have a friend is to be one.*
> Ralph Waldo Emerson

### What Should Be Absent in a Spiritual Workplace?

Since the vital factors for a spiritual workplace become even clearer if we also emphasize those types of behavior that should be absent in the spiritual workplace, we now present our findings on what the people we interviewed during recent years felt about this issue. Table 3.2 presents the most frequently used words for elements absent in a spiritually nurtured workplace.

Table 3.2. What should be absent in a spiritual workplace?

| Factors: | |
| --- | --- |
| Negativity | Dishonesty |
| Excessive Control | Strong Hierarchy |
| Egocentric Behavior | Backstabbing |
| Mistrust | |

## Vital Themes for a Spiritual Workplace

Table 3.3 below lists the themes vital to a spiritual workplace that we culled from all of our interviews.

Table 3.3. Vital themes.

| Themes | |
| --- | --- |
| Ethics | Trust |
| Truth | Kindness (bonding, conviviality, compassion) |
| Belief in God or a higher power | Team Orientation |
| Respect | Few organizational barriers |
| Understanding | A sense of peace and harmony |
| Openness | Aesthetically pleasing workplace |
| Honesty | Interconnectedness |
| Being self-motivated | Encouraging diversity |
| Encourage creativity | Acceptance |
| Giving to others | |

## Findings from the Themes

As explained earlier, the phrases listed in Table 3.3 were predominantly extracted from the common themes we discovered during our research. If we review these themes from a business perspective, we find that, with the exception of *Belief in God or a higher power*, all the themes simply pertain to good organizational behavior and responsible management as described by various management theorists. In fact, even the *Belief in God or a higher power* theme can be related to good management principles, since the majority of our interviewees chose to generally refer to a "higher source" or a "higher power." Seen from this angle, this particular theme could be interpreted as what is commonly known as drive or internal motivation, also very much in line with generally recommended management principles. We can therefore conclude that the greatest part of the important themes mentioned by the participants in this study refer to good managerial practices and leadership behavior as the basic elements of a spiritual workplace.

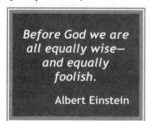

*Before God we are all equally wise— and equally foolish.*

Albert Einstein

Considering the fact that so many business executives still have an aversion to the term spirituality in the workplace, it becomes even more noteworthy that the interviewees in our studies mentioned such strong organizational behavioral themes as the most significant ones. This finding strengthens the insight that spirituality in the workplace has nothing to do with ethereal experiences or states, but everything to do with proper organizational behavior involving humane approaches toward one another. As a consequence, we can state that spirituality in the workplace has everything to do with good organizational performance, and, in contradiction to what business executives fear, with a better positioning of the organization overall, a more solid and more reliable workforce, and greater return on investment. These findings are in harmony with the results of a recent mainstream study linking organizational performance with spirituality in the workplace.(36)

## Review of the Themes

We will now briefly review how the various themes fit into a spiritual workplace:

### Ethics
*Ethics* forms an essential part of a spiritual workplace. It should not only be seen as a crucial element for every spiritual worker, but also for the workplace as a whole, and ultimately for the entire network the workplace operates in. It is important to emphasize that mere instruction or review of ethics will not contribute to the level of spirituality in the workplace if the individuals involved do not integrate the value into their sense of spirituality. It is an experiential process—the application of this tendency among leaders and employees—that will determine the successful application of this factor.

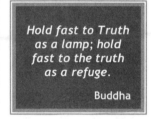

> *Hold fast to Truth as a lamp; hold fast to the truth as a refuge.*
>
> Buddha

### Truth
The word *truth* can be interpreted in at least two different ways: 1) in the sense of "understanding the real intentions behind one's remarks"; and 2) as a phenomenon that needs to be part of the making of the spiritual workplace, as well as a substitute for the word *honesty*.

### Belief in a higher power
When we perceive the expression *a higher power*, we see a certain level of discrepancy in the way various people view it; while some may plainly refer to their belief in God from a religious perspective, others may prefer to remain general by referring to "a higher source." Yet others may choose to perceive this higher power as an inner drive. This perceptual diffusion is an excellent demonstration why spirituality

should not be confused with religion, particularly not in the workplace. The leader in a spiritual workplace should acknowledge and respect the various viewpoints of his or her employees without showing any preference for one particular perspective.

## Respect
The main distinction in perceptions in this regard may be that, while some people feel that respect should occur reciprocally among colleagues, others may refer to this theme as an emotion that needs to be maintained toward the entire environment, encompassing other people, as well as mother nature in its entirety.

*It is well to give when asked but it is better to give unasked, through understanding.*

Kahlil Gibran

## Understanding
The theme *understanding* can also be interpreted in different ways: While most people may link this factor to the sense of comprehending at a deeper level, some may also use the word in the context of *appreciation*. Some people may even think of the art of surviving, which makes us appreciative and understanding toward the true source of our blessings; and others may mention understanding together with *caring* and *fairness* as basic premises in an organization. In any case, understanding has an undercurrent of acceptance and gratitude, as opposed to the normal perspective of just comprehending. This, then, may well be the best way to perceive the concept of understanding when considering spirituality at work.

## Openness
Although *openness* may commonly mean *being receptive and flexible* in the context of work environment, some people may also consider openness as an organizational reciprocity, whereby you should think more in terms of accessibility within the organization toward its employees. This kind of openness, then, would include prerequisites such as a free flow of communication and reduction of barriers.

## Honesty
The majority of people may initially perceive the word *honesty* as a trait projected from oneself toward others. However, some also mention honesty as a cultural goal—an atmosphere that can be created by a leader who wants to enhance the level of spiritual awareness in his or her workplace.

## Being self-motivated
*Self-motivation* is mainly thought of as an internal quality of the spiritual worker. When talking about self-motivation, some people may

also include possible sources that can harness this internal emotion such as openness, respect, and a supportive culture characterized by mutual understanding.

### Encourage creativity
This refers to providing opportunities and venues for developing unique skills, and making the best out of every situation. Some people may add to this perspective the necessity of finding creative alternatives or solutions to problems, since this, too, can be interpreted as *creativity*.

### Giving to others
In the context of workplace spirituality, people primarily use the word *giving* in the sense of sharing something with co-workers, whether it pertains to mundane or spiritual guidance offered in terms of one's total commitment or support offered in times of need.

### Trust
*Trust* is usually emphasized as the glue that binds the spiritual workplace together. It manifests itself on three levels: 1) within the spiritual worker; 2) among all employees and throughout the organization, leading to greater accessibility; and 3) between the organization and the community in which it operates.

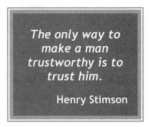

*The only way to make a man trustworthy is to trust him.*

Henry Stimson

Because of the many ways it can be interpreted, many people consider this theme one of the basic building blocks of a spiritual workplace.

### Kindness
*Kindness* refers to a caring concern for the well-being of others. There seems to be overwhelming similarity in perspectives on kindness. People generally agree that kindness is a common practice in a spiritual workplace.

### Team orientation
The *team* factor is also predominantly underscored as highly significant in a spiritual work setting, although it may be mentioned in various ways. Most people emphasize team spirit as the most effective way of eliminating barriers, getting rid of rigid hierarchical structures, celebrating diversity, and encouraging accessibility.

### Few organizational barriers
When mentioning *few organizational barriers* in the context of workplace spirituality, many people explain this in the sense of accessibility to information, approachability to people from various departments and at various levels, and the advantage that accessibility brings to the decision-making process: a sense of purpose, which

encourages the spiritual worker to think more in terms of the overall organization due to an increased understanding of where his or her contribution fits in the bigger picture.

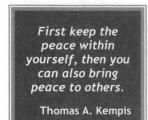

*First keep the peace within yourself, then you can also bring peace to others.*

Thomas A. Kempis

### A sense of peace and harmony
This statement may trigger an interesting diversity of opinions, although there may be general agreement with the idea that peace and harmony are important cornerstones of a spiritual workplace. But while some people may consider *peace* as part of the work environment (atmosphere-related), others may prefer to look at it as a human emotion (contentment-related).

### Aesthetically pleasing workplace
Of course the idea of what is aesthetically pleasing may vary from one person to another. Yet, it seems that there is an interesting discrepancy in perspectives between males and females in this regard: while most females may perceive an *aesthetically pleasant environment* as one decorated with plants and accompanied by soft music and a pleasant smell, male executives may mainly refer to people and behavioral patterns in a work environment as determining factors of the atmosphere.

### Interconnectedness
*Interconnectedness* is yet another term that may invite an interesting diversity in perceptions. We may stumble upon the perspective of inter-connection versus the idea of inner-connection. While most people may relate to interconnectedness among spiritual workers as advantageous to their performance and, hence, the overall welfare of the spiritual workplace, some may add a different dimension to this issue; for instance, interconnectedness may be seen as the more reflexive condition of inner-connectedness.

### Encouraging diversity
The suggestion most people make here is that there should be respect for difference of opinion in a spiritual workplace, because *encouragement of diversity* generally leads to better input and, hence, improved output. Diversity seen from this viewpoint is a favorite theme of management theorists. However, a number of people may feel that diversity in a spiritual workplace should also be seen in light of respect for differences and new organizational developments.

## Acceptance

*Acceptance* may be seen as one of the main foundations of a spiritual workplace. The previously evaluated themes of respect, understanding, openness, honesty, encouragement, giving, trust, kindness, team orientation, few organizational barriers, a sense of peace and harmony, interconnectedness, and encouraging diversity, all require acceptance in order to be possible.

> *Of course there is no formula for success except perhaps an unconditional acceptance of life and what it brings.*
>
> Arthur Rubinstein

It may be important for us to reemphasize at this point that, although the themes listed above characterize the interaction among employees in a spiritual workplace, they are definitely also part of the interaction between leaders and employees, as well as between leaders and all other stakeholders.

## In Review

It is clear from the information gathered from our studies that spirituality in the workplace is an experience that can only exist if all essential factors are in harmony with each other. The majority of our sources (literature and interviews) seemed to be in agreement with the need for collaboration by all stakeholders at all levels in creating a spiritual workplace.

The main term used to express this need is *interconnectedness*. Here are some example statements regarding interconnectedness made by various participants we interviewed:

- Spiritual needs are fulfilled by a recognition and acceptance of individual responsibility for the common good, by understanding the interconnectedness of all life, and by serving humanity and the planet.(37)
- We are interconnected to all life.(38)
- Spirituality is the deep feeling of the interconnectedness of everything.(39)
- People have that spiritual connection, you know?
- If you are relating to that power within, that is all-powerful, all-knowing, everywhere present, and connecting with its wholeness, and you become one with its wholeness...[and] with everything that you come in contact with—*then* you experience interconnectedness.
- I think there is this connectivity, and I therefore think an environment should be created in an organization where people

could particularly talk about it. So that should be looked at and capitalized on.

In sum, based on the statements by the people we interviewed during our studies, as well as literature reviewed, spirituality in the workplace requires:

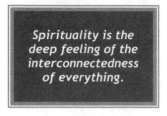

*Spirituality is the deep feeling of the interconnectedness of everything.*

1. A set of personal factors within each individual who wants to operate at his or her highest level of spiritual awareness;
2. A set of externally applicable factors that this person needs to maintain a high sense of spirituality with others in his or her environment;
3. A set of factors that the organization as an entity should have to maintain and apply internally to garner greater spirituality in the workplace;
4. A set of factors that the organization as an entity should have to apply externally;
5. A set of emergent experiences that should flow back to the spiritual worker.

Based on more recent updates to our study, we generated the following confirmation of previous findings, which may serve as an effective conclusion of this chapter.

**Spirituality in the workplace entails:**

- A focus on quality of life for employees, quality of output, and efficiency of processes;
- More focus on the personal and spiritual connectedness between organization and employees' goals;
- Shifting the paradigm in all sectors of endeavor:
  - o From top-down hierarchy to a lateral organization characterized by mentoring-trusting-sharing-teaming;
  - o From simple bottom line outcomes to exploring sustainable horizons that address complex problems and processes through time-honored and group-determined guiding principles;
  - o Seeking viable connections among and across various disciplines and areas of knowledge;
  - o Willingness to probe for deeper levels of truth and creative solutions;
  - o Tolerance for risk-taking and ambiguity;
- Evaluating and seeking to understand ourselves both as individuals and as a part of the web of our interrelationships with

others, by starting within and extending out to both the workplace and the world. Also, as individuals, trying to develop trust and goodwill through understanding, honesty, kindness, love, and respect for others;

- Seeking an answer to the age-old question of the meaning of our lives on this planet as we are caught up in a frenetically accelerating and increasingly complex postindustrial world;
- Encouragement of:
  o A sense of personal possibilities;
  o A willingness to recognize personal possibilities in others;
  o A personal and work environment where this recognition can occur;
- Sincerely and wisely embracing, nurturing, and honoring the full potential of individuals in the organization, thereby engaging more fully their personal power to achieve their own as well as their organization's purposes. It also entails looking at the organization as one whole system, together with people who comprise it.

> *Spirituality in the workplace entails more focus on the personal and spiritual connectedness between organization and employees' goals.*

## Spirituality in the workplace does NOT entail:

- A mere focus on the bottom line;
- Micromanaging;
- Excessive focus on economic effects that are not reflective of problems that arise in the industry;
- A top-down hierarchy;
- A checklist mentality to simply manipulate situations to achieve profit and/or material outcomes without careful consideration of the impact on environmental, human, and organic systems, short-term and long-term;
- Ruthless competition, cruelty, secrecy, dishonesty, greed, irresponsibility, backbiting, gossip or slander, negativity, pitting one person against another, favoritism, and lastly, the need to win or achieve one's goal at any cost;
- Quantifying success only in terms of corporate or personal financial return or productivity of hours spent at work;
- Dishonest rewards, even those intended to encourage;
- Any wild-eyed adherence to an offbeat philosophy.

As you may have already concluded, the findings from subsequent studies are in close agreement with previous conclusions presented earlier in this chapter.

> *A sense of duty is useful in work, but offensive in personal relations. People wish to be liked, not be endured with patient resignation.*
>
> Bertrand Russell

## Reflection Sheet

These areas represent the contents of this chapter that I consider applicable to my life:

_____
_____
_____
_____
_____
_____
_____

These areas represent the contents of this chapter whose applicability to my life I question:

_____
_____
_____
_____
_____
_____
_____
_____

My personal opinions after reading this chapter:

_____
_____
_____
_____
_____

What I would like to remember:

_____
_____
_____
_____
_____
_____

# Part II

## Spirituality in the Workplace: Why it Matters

### Facts and Effects

# Chapter 4

# The
# Diversity
# Factor

This chapter focuses on the positive aspects of diversity in the workplace, and the necessity of management and human resource departments to not only identify the importance of workplace diversity, but to implement and accommodate diversity at every level in the work environment as well. Even though there is a wide range of arguments to be listed in this regard, the focus in this chapter will be limited to the following advantages of workforce diversity, as seen within the scope of workplace spirituality:

- Feeling good by doing the right thing;
- Creating a better work environment while providing improved service to customers;
- Making the organization more innovative, productive, and creative;
- Increasing employees' commitment by practicing more flexibility;
- Enhancing employees' inter-human skills as a tool for lasting future career success.

We will discuss these points of focus in the course of this chapter.

ecause the issues to be reviewed are applicable to practically every work environment, it is logical that they also apply to those workplaces that consider themselves spiritual.

### Diversity Defined

According to David DeCenzo and Stephen Robbins, diversity means recognizing, respecting, and celebrating differences in people. Work force diversity includes the varied backgrounds of employees that are present in our companies today.(40) Predicting our future work force diversity, DeCenzo and Robins, established authorities in human resource management, explained that they will be made up of males, females, whites, blacks, Hispanics, Asians, Native Americans, the disabled, homosexuals, straights, and the elderly.(41) Increasingly, this picture becomes visible in workplaces throughout the globe.

*Diversity is the one true thing we all have in common. Celebrate it every day.*

Anonymous

DeCenzo and Robbins stated that anyone who is not sensitive to diversity issues needs to stop and check his or her attitude at the door.

53

These authors predicted quite some time ago that by the end of the 90s, people of color, white women, and immigrants would account for 85 percent of our labor force.(42) Their predictions have turned out to be fairly accurate.

## The Current Situation

It is a somewhat discouraging fact that, whenever diversity is implemented in today's workplaces, it still seems to be for all but the right reason—enhancing advantage for the organization as well as its individuals. In most of today's workplaces it is only the organization that benefits whenever diversity is implemented. In a few cases, diversity is merely applied for moral reasons, perhaps even tying in with top management's religious beliefs or sensitivity toward affirmative action.

In most of these organizations, diversity is only applied at the visible level, that is, at lower- and mid-level layers of the organization, but not at the top, where the picture oftentimes remains fairly homogeneous, consisting of older white males.

> The most universal quality is diversity.
>
> Michel Eyquem De Montaigne

In these organizations, the perspective that diversity can lead to greater advancement for the organization is entirely overlooked. These workplaces fail to consider diversity-related benefits such as the quality of output and the organization's place in its industry. They also fail to consider how diversity benefits employees by learning from one another, becoming more flexible in handling problems in the future, and improving personally in multiple environments.

Below are some factors that a spiritual workplace should consider as a total package when applying diversity.

## Feeling Good by Doing the Right Thing

DeCenzo and Robbins cite Connie Sitterly, who makes a very strong point for diversity. In Sitterly's opinion, implementing workplace diversity should be done not only because it is the law, or because it is morally and ethically the right thing to do, or because it makes good business sense, but also because when we open our minds and hearts, we feel better about ourselves.(43)

This brings us to the first, and maybe most important, advantage of diversity within the scope of establishing a more spiritually attuned workplace. This advantage ensues by way of establishing a feeling of satisfaction, because the choice has been made to do the right thing, as opposed to taking the easy way out by hiring people who make the easiest fit, given their similarities in backgrounds, education, thought processes, religious convictions, age groups, or sexual orientation.

Another author, Michael Verespej, agrees that the problem is often not whether companies can find someone who is qualified; it is whether they think someone will fit in. According to Verespej, companies try to make people fit, rather than creating a work environment where people can feel comfortable and contribute regardless of their backgrounds or culture. Verespej discusses a fable told by Roosevelt Thomas Jr., CEO of R. Thomas Consulting & Training Inc., about the friendship and subsequent business partnership between a giraffe and an elephant. Problems arise when the elephant tries to fit into the giraffe's house. The story subsequently explains that elephants should not be forced to fit in giraffes' houses, but rather be accommodated in an environment that fits their shape as well as the giraffes', resulting in a general feeling of comfort and increased performance. Verespej clarifies his point by citing former U.S. Secretary of Labor Lynn Martin, who stated:

> You can't treat people the same. That is not how you manage diversity. The single biggest mistake we in management can make is to say that sameness is equality. Understanding and managing diversity means listening to someone else even if you don't like what you hear.(44)

### Better Work Environment, Better Customer Service

In an article published in summer 2000 by the International Personnel Management Association, Jacqueline Gilbert stated that the advantage for the American industry in the world market will be based on our success in optimizing and utilizing a richly diverse work force. According to Gilbert, this prediction suggests that to succeed in the future, organizations must learn how to attract, promote, and retain a diverse group of people in order to sustain a competitive advantage.(45) Dianah Worman, resident equal opportunities guru for the Chartered Institute of Personnel and Development (CIPD), underlines this opinion by explaining that it is in the employers' interest to think smartly about who their potential workers are; a sophisticated approach to customers and clients outside the

> *The advantage for the American industry in the world market will be based upon our success in optimizing and utilizing a richly diverse work force.*
>
> Jacqueline Gilbert

organization should be mirrored in the way employers approach their staffing.(46)

Jonathan Alger asserted that the argument for the necessity of diversity is perhaps stronger in higher education than in any other context:

> The ultimate product of universities is education in the broadest sense, including preparation for life in the working world. As part of this education, students learn from face-to-face interaction with faculty members and with one another both inside and outside the classroom. Racial diversity can enhance this interaction by broadening course offerings, texts, and classroom examples, as well as improving communications and understanding among individuals of different races.(47)

In a more general sense, Charlotte Thomas stated in an article specifically devoted to the topic of hiring minorities that diversity is about bringing different perspectives to the company. She further explained that the next challenge will be to improve diversity at higher levels. Once that perspective is in place, said Thomas, there will be more mentors and role models creating a win-win situation for both individual employees and the corporation as a whole.(48)

### Innovativeness, Productivity, and Creativity

Orlando Richard and Nancy Johnson explained that a diversity orientation results in a diverse culture where employees embrace their differences and use them to enhance organizational effectiveness through creativity and innovation. Diversity practices can provide firms with the expertise to regularly develop and market competitive new products by enhancing organizational creativity and problem solving. According to Richard and Johnson, the relationship between diversity orientation and performance is contingent on an organization's business strategy, but also on the organization's human resource strategy.

> *Diversity practices can provide firms with the expertise to regularly develop and market competitive new products by enhancing organizational creativity and problem solving.*
>
> Orlando Richard and Nancy Johnson

With this statement Richard and Johnson explain that much of the implementation and success of workforce diversity depends on the priorities on which an organization's human resource department focuses. With these priorities aiming at better long-term performance rather than lower immediate costs, diversity will be accommodated and proven successful. Richard and Johnson predict that the levels of racial and gender diversity and diversity orientation will positively affect organizational performance through their interaction. This makes perfect sense: where minds from different backgrounds meet, there will be more creative outcomes, of a higher quality, and with a longer lasting impact. However, Richard and Johnson warn that these performance outcomes occur over time. A group's ability to embrace and leverage diversity usually emerges slowly.(49)

## Increase Employee's Commitment by Practicing More Flexibility

Worman exclaims that most employees are so grateful for that extra bit of flexibility you give them, that they actually become even more committed. Worman believes that developing work/life policies to meet the needs of a diverse workforce must begin with an understanding of the inherent value of diversity. She firmly holds the opinion that a healthy approach to flexible working will bring benefits not just for employees, but for businesses too.(50) Worman's point of view is shared by Richard and Johnson, who also note that effective diversity management enhances organizational flexibility, simply because more diverse groups consider a wider variety of perspectives. As diversity policies and practices become instituted, increased fluidity and flexibility result in an organizational culture that can react to environmental changes(51).

> *Effective diversity management enhances organizational flexibility, simply because more diverse groups consider a wider variety of perspectives.*
>
> Orlando Richard and Nancy Johnson

## Enhance Employees' Inter-Human Skills as a Tool for Lasting Future Career Success

One aspect that should not be underestimated is the well-being of employees, not only while they are part of the current work environment, but during their entire career. Exposing people to diversity enlarges their horizons; opens their mind for alternative methods and insights, and increases their sense of acceptance toward one another. This makes employees better equipped for future changes in the global work environment and protects them from shocks that may occur when situations alter tremendously.

Managers who are genuinely concerned about the advancement of employees, whether in their current workplace or elsewhere, are truly spiritual leaders. These spiritual leaders thus elevate their scope beyond the status quo and strive toward lasting betterment of employees under all circumstances. These spiritual leaders are also aware that when employees realize that supervisors have their best interests at heart, turnover will decrease. For who wants to leave a workplace where managers are not just interested in output, but also in the long-term well-being of their employees?

## The Responsibility of Human Resources in Diversity

In an article published in *HR Magazine* in 2001, Lin Grensing-Pophal asked the interesting question, "If an organization says it is committed to diversity and is attempting to build a diverse workforce, should its HR [human resources] staff not exemplify diversity in its own ranks?"

While enumerating the advantages of workforce diversity in the above-mentioned article, Grensing-Pophal emphasized that any HR (human resources) department should also have as much diversity as possible. Grensing-Pophal exclaims that when it comes to diversity, the HR department is viewed as a leader in the organization. "If they don't do it, other departments will say it's not possible." In Grensing-Pophal's opinion, it is very important from a credibility point of view that the people who work in the HR department are reflective of the workforce at large and that they understand the diversity of their internal customers.(52)

> *If an organization says it is committed to diversity and is attempting to build a diverse workforce, should its HR staff not exemplify diversity in its own ranks?*
>
> Lin Grensing-Pophal

Richard and Johnson add that diversity depends on human resource policies that are judged and evaluated by employees in a context dependent upon organizational justice perceptions. Richard and Johnson feel that human resource policies and practices that fit with the business strategies of the firm enhance firm effectiveness.(53)

## In Review

Although there are various negative aspects to be considered when implementing workforce diversity such as increased costs, higher employee turnover in the initial stages, and slower initial corporate progress due to diversity-related misunderstandings, this chapter presented a brief overview of the various advantages of workforce diversity in an increasingly diverse global workplace. As stated in the introduction, all of the advantages as well as the possible disadvantages of workforce diversity, are applicable to all work environments.

In many of the articles cited it was stated that diversity is not a naturally preferred process, because people have a tendency to hire others who are like themselves.(54)

This is somewhat understandable; especially when corporations are looking for short-term output increase. However, it will be those who implement diversity now and create a work-environment that brings out the best in a diverse workforce who enjoy the profits of this strategic decision in the long run. As Richard and Johnson state, projections show that increasing diversity in the workplace is a reality, not a myth,(55) and since the student body in many higher educational institutions is diverse, and since the customer base of many for-profit and not-for-profit organizations is also diverse, one should not underestimate the importance of association: a student or customer who can find at least one staff, faculty, or sales force member like him- or herself, will feel more "at home."

In sum, if conscientiously applied and facilitated at all levels, diversity can elevate an organization's long-term performance to levels that surpass all expectations. The implementation of diversity for the right reasons should become a first priority with consideration of the following factors:

- The increasing diversification of the local workforce;
- Organizations' need to search for more advantageous markets and production unit locations outside their current comfort zone;
- The continuous increase of organizational stakeholder bases due to enhanced global accessibility.

Figure 4.1 on the next page provides an interesting summary of the points made in this chapter.

> *It will be those who implement diversity now and create a work-environment that brings out the best in a diverse workforce who enjoy the profits of this strategic decision in the long run.*

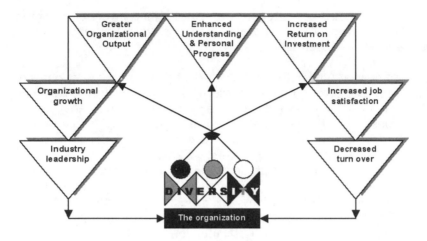

Figure 4.1. The effects of applying diversity in a workplace.

## Reflection Sheet

These areas represent the contents of this chapter that I consider applicable to my life:

These areas represent the contents of this chapter whose applicability to my life I question:

My personal opinions after reading this chapter:

What I would like to remember:

# Chapter 5

# Organizational Resilience

This chapter will review the consequences that the application of spiritual practices (not to be confused with religious practices) has on the workplace. In this part of the book we will illustrate how organizations with the right set of approaches can reinvent themselves repeatedly, either within one industry, or in various industries over time. Subsequently, we will take a closer look into the phenomenon of organizational culture and how this can influence the organization's performance.

## The Spiritual Organization as Revolutionary

S*pirituality* and *revolutionary* may sound fairly paradoxical in one sentence, particularly when linked in a cooperative context. Yet, the pairing should make sense after we get the definitions straight and ascertain how the two topics relate in this chapter.

Spirituality in the workplace, as stated above in Chapter 1, is not the same as religion in the workplace. Religion is something we can all make a choice about. We can change religions from one day to another. We can choose to be non-religious. And we should definitely not be forced to put up with other people's religion.

> *If man does find the solution for world peace it will be the most revolutionary reversal of his record we have ever known.*
>
> George C. Marshall

As Rosner stated so well, and as we explicitly mentioned in Chapter 1, there is a difference between religion and spirituality, and you can provide for a spiritual work environment without forcing a particular religious point of view down anyone's throat.(56)

Or, like Alex Paterson asserted, "Religion and spirituality are often confused with each other, yet in many respects religion has very little to do with spirituality and everything to do with the attainment of secular power and wealth for rather base and venal reasons."(57)

Religions often present an over-simplistic and narrow view of reality; they are often intolerant of contrary views and prone to demeaning the basic tenets underlying spirituality in their attempts to present a finite and limited interpretation of the infinite. Spirituality, on the other hand, usually entails a far deeper personal experience associated with an individual's personal quest to rediscover his or her essence and who he or she really is (i.e. the essence of one's identity). We could therefore explain spirituality as something we all carry within us: our pure selves, our sense for self-respect and respect for others.

To reiterate from Chapter 1, we define spirituality in the workplace as

> *an experience of interconnectedness among those involved in a work process, initiated by authenticity, reciprocity, and personal goodwill; engendered by a deep sense of meaning that is inherent in the organization's work; and resulting in greater motivation and organizational excellence.*

Simply put, spirituality in the workplace is that "at home" feeling that we all should have doing our daily job: a great level of comfort, intermingled with a great level of responsibility. After all, is that not what being at home is all about? While we feel at ease, we also know that it is all about us. *We* matter! Our opinion, our input, our presence, our entire being is appreciated and makes a difference. And because we realize that, we care. Being heard and having ownership makes us feel that what we do is worthwhile. And that is the whole point of having a spiritual workplace that ultimately becomes a "gray-haired revolutionary."(58)

> *In a time of universal deceit, telling the truth will be a revolutionary act.*
>
> George Orwell

For further explanation of the gray-haired *revolutionary*, we look to strategic management expert Gary Hamel, who used the term to describe a company that has managed to reinvent itself and its industry more than once—a company that goes by some kind of unwritten but commonly understood and practiced rule, such as, "whatever is the real deal at the moment, that's what we're specializing in."(59)

A gray-haired revolutionary, according to Hamel, is an organization that realizes that strategies are not immortal phenomena—they are subject to change like anything else, that is, if they hope to survive in today's fast changing world! We see very few CEOs who have the capability of coming up with successful new visions more than once in a lifetime. Even if you have yet to read or listened to Hamel, you will probably agree that CEOs seldom exhibit 20/20 foresight when predicting what will be hot tomorrow. But what the CEO often fails to see, others can! That is why everybody in the organization should matter, because at other levels, especially the operational, there are people who would also like to be heard, who may have great ideas about what would work, who regularly hear about what clients and customers would like to see changed.

Imagine what could happen to a company if the fieldworkers were given an opportunity to convey their findings and opinions to the top levels of the organization; if *they* were considered—people with brains—not machines that are shut down at 5:00 p.m. Discerning managers can see that workers tend to react with irresponsible and uncaring behavior when they are treated like machines, expected to perform with no consideration of what is right or wrong. This is very much in line with Chris Argyris' perspective of Theory X managers, who consider workers to be negative, unwilling, and irresponsible creatures, as opposed to Theory Y managers, who consider workers as responsible, willing, and able partners. In both cases, according to Argyris, management will reap what it sows, because both concepts are self-fulfilling prophecies. People often respond just as they are expected to!

So how can an organization's management expect any sense of ownership, responsibility, or loyalty from workers whom it regards negatively? What hope could management hold out for employees to offer solutions to problems that might seem insurmountable to the boss, even though the employees are, in fact, the experts who should be consulted?

A gray-haired revolutionary works entirely in the opposite direction. In such an organization, all employees have a voice, even if in a structured and organized way. Because there is good communication, it is a workplace where people feel that they matter, their thoughts concerning processes at work are heard and considered, and their family needs are appreciated. It is a workplace where there is a connection between top management and the

> The main reason that today's workforce predominantly behaves irresponsibly and seems uncaring is because for years on end, they were expected to behave like machines and to do the job without thinking what was right or wrong.

operational level without 50 doors that separate them. It is a workplace where everyone wants to stay, and management makes it possible to stay. So every idea, every vision, every hunch, is shared for the benefit of the community. The company can reinvent itself countless times, and workers are content because they find meaning in what they do. It is a spiritual workplace. But it reinvents itself time and again, so it is a revolutionary as well. That is how spirituality in the workplace facilitates gray-haired revolutionaries.

## The Interdependency Among Organizational Culture, Performance, and Productivity

Following our discussion of the relationship between spirituality and revolutionary behavior, a further examination of the connection among an organization's culture, its performance, and its output is in order. First and foremost, the nature of an organization's culture has everything to do with its performance, and, hence, its productivity level. As mentioned above, a motivational culture guarantees openness, accessibility, respect, and acceptance at all levels, facilitating a greater sense of unity among employees and stakeholders, and, consequently, a greater enthusiasm in the organization to perform with excellence. This part of the chapter will review the phenomenal nature of organizational culture, performance, and productivity in order to establish evidence of their interdependency.

Management theorist Ed Schein defined culture as "the sum total of what a given group has learned as a group, embodied in a set of shared, basic underlying assumptions that are no longer conscious, but are taken for granted as the way the world is." Narrowing culture down to the organizational level, Schein saw organizational culture as a pattern of basic assumptions that a given group has invented, discovered, or developed in learning to cope with its problems of external adaptation and internal integration. Furthermore, these assumptions have worked well enough to be considered valid, and, therefore, are taught to new members as the correct way to perceive, think, and feel in relation to those problems. (60)

> *Organizational culture: a system of shared beliefs and values that develops within an organization and guides the behaviors of its members.*
>
> **Angelo Kinicki and Brian Williams**

Angelo Kinicki and Brian Williams presented a concise version of Schein's definition in their description of organizational culture as "a system of shared beliefs and values that develops within an organization and guides the behaviors of its members."(61) Incorporated in this definition is the essence of the impact an organization's culture can have on its performance and productivity, and hence, its bottom line. Interestingly, business executives and scholars still seem to view the impact of culture on production with skepticism; it is, therefore, essential to first define the terms involved in this relationship before further analysis of the relationship itself.

## A Closer Look at Organizational Culture

An organization's culture can manifest itself at two levels, according to Kinicki and Williams:

1. The invisible level, which mainly pertains to the core culture of values and beliefs as defined by Schein above;
2. The visible level, which pertains to the ways people dress, the layout of the workplace, the slogans, symbols, stories, heroes, rites, and rituals of the organization. (62)

John Schermerhorn emphasized that, at any level, these values should meet the test of the following three criteria:

1. Relevance (core values should support key performance objectives);
2. Pervasiveness (core values should be known by all members of the organization or group);
3. Strength (core values should be accepted by everyone involved). (63)

From the above, we can easily conclude that the visible culture is inspired by the invisible culture. Organizations that demonstrate a strong participative approach encouraged by the leaders toward all echelons, great accessibility at all levels, and an atmosphere of sensitivity and hospitality, tend to display a more relaxed dress code whenever and wherever appropriate. Further, such organizations exhibit enhanced, pleasant, friendly, and laid-back relationships among employees, and between employees and other stakeholders such as suppliers and customers. These organizations are increasingly referred to as spiritual workplaces, although some dislike the label due to general misconceptions in regard to the word *spiritual*, which, as described above, is often confused with religion or other ethereal concepts that seem inappropriate in a business setting.

### Organizational performance

Organizational performance can be described as the degree to which an organization achieves its goals. This implies that there can be good, bad, and mediocre organizational performance. It requires no specification that the organizational goals should be set at a challenging yet achievable level, neither too high nor too low. Yet, unachievable goals are discouraging to the company spirit, whereas easy goals result in mediocre performance. An organization's goals are captured in the corporate strategy. It is vital that employees at all

> *Organizational performance: the degree to which an organization achieves its goals.*

levels of the organization know at least the main thread of the corporate strategy in order to achieve a sense of meaning in their work through understanding of its purpose. In other words, employees should be aware of the bigger picture: what they are really doing here; whom they are serving; where they are going; why their job is important.

> *When workers are aware of the ultimate essence of their daily efforts, they will feel more engaged in the process.*

The four main terms that surfaced in the above paragraph are 1) performance; 2) goals; 3) strategies; and 4) employees. This foursome in and of its own is a logical sequence, in that the organization will perform better if its goals are clear, challenging, yet achievable, laid out in an understandable strategy, and familiar to employees at all levels. It is only when employees are aware of the bigger picture of their activities—when they know what the ultimate essence is of their daily efforts—that they feel more engaged in the process, take ownership, and perform at their highest capacities. When employees perform to their highest capacities—assuming, of course, that skills, tools, and motivation are also in place—organizational performance increases.

### Productivity
Productivity can simply be defined as outputs divided by inputs. Outputs, according to Kinicki and Williams, are all the goods and services produced. Inputs entail the labor, capital, materials, and energy.

Kinicki and Williams portrayed the equation of productivity as follows:

$$productivity = \frac{outputs}{inputs} \quad or \quad \frac{goods + services}{labor + capital + materials + energy}$$

Obviously, productivity is crucial to companies, determining ultimately whether the organization will make a profit or even survive. (64)

If we link the two earlier described phenomena, organizational culture and performance, to the above equation, we can come to the following analysis:

### Inputs
- *Labor*, the workforce, needs to be aware of the bigger picture—the organization's goals and strategy—in order to feel integrated and motivated. This will inspire greater levels of individual and group performance, and, hence, greater input.

- Although *capital* is predominantly an input element controlled by top management and shareholders, there is an emerging trend of companies selling stocks to employees, making them co-owners of the corporation. This is not only a smart way to generate capital, but it is also a great way of increasing employees' motivation and connectedness toward optimal performance of the company they co-own.

- The pursuit of *materials* involves suppliers. A company with a hospitable approach toward suppliers stands to benefit from reciprocal positive relations from the suppliers, which can often include profitable network or discount programs that link the suppliers' customers for efficiency purposes.

- *Energy* may not be perceived as a factor directly influenced by enhanced performance, but a more streamlined approach in the workforce and better planned sequences in production can lead to more responsible energy use and, thus, decreased energy expenses.

## Outputs

- While the *goods* and *services* the company delivers become more affordable for customers in a more streamlined approach on the input side, the quality increases as well due to better communication among employees, unified efforts, and a general team spirit. Both of these advantages, lower prices and higher quality, are important tools toward the organization's establishment of enhanced competitive advantage.

Overall, productivity requires control from the company's leaders. This control should be executed in a manner that is motivating and facilitating rather than degrading and restricting. Regular meetings, cross-functional teams, process overview sessions, idea encouragement programs, and performance rewards are integral to top management's control of productivity through positive motivation and facilitation.

*When people feel "at home" while at work, they dare to take more responsibility, which will positively affect the bottom line.*

### The bottom line

Indeed, business organizations exist for the purpose of profitability. That is a statement we hear time and again, to which we offer no argument but this: the bottom-line can become even more rewarding when organizational leaders foster a culture that enhances connectivity among employees. By now, this connectivity factor has been given many names: spirituality in the workplace, values-based performance, team orientation, or simply *good management*. All of these terms entail a common theme: making people feel "at home" while at work, so that they dare to take ownership, feel responsibility, enjoy their time at the workplace, and perform at a level that will ensure the longevity of their "work-home."

## In Review

In this chapter, we explained the close relationship between two seemingly contradictory terms in organizations: spirituality and revolution. Through simple analysis of both terms, we arrived at the conclusion that spiritual workplaces are in fact the most revolutionary ones, because employees are more involved, and will, henceforth, do everything to keep their workplace afloat and, preferably, prosperous. This will be the case particularly if they also share in the greater well-being of the organization.

> *An organization that harbors a culture of communication without barriers will reach continuously higher performance levels and enjoy amplified growth.*

To clarify the interaction between an organization's spirituality and its performance, we subsequently reviewed the interdependency among organizational culture, performance, and productivity to arrive at the conclusion that an organization that harbors a culture of open communication without barriers will reach continuously higher performance levels, because productivity will increase as inputs amplify and outputs consequently augment the bottom line. As profits increase, the organization gains growth capacity.

# Reflection Sheet

These areas represent the contents of this chapter that I consider applicable to my life:

_____
_____
_____
_____
_____
_____
_____
_____

These areas represent the contents of this chapter whose applicability to my life I question:

_____
_____
_____
_____
_____
_____
_____
_____
_____
_____

My personal opinions after reading this chapter:

_____
_____
_____
_____
_____
_____
_____

What I would like to remember:

_____
_____
_____
_____
_____
_____
_____

# Chapter 6

# Value Added
## to the
# Bottom Line

In this chapter we elaborate on an issue that is most important to business managers and CEOs—the bottom line. Many still question the relationship between spirituality in the workplace and the organization's return on investment.

One of the main reasons there is hesitance toward spirit at work is because there is still too much unfamiliarity with what the phenomenon really entails. Because spirituality in the workplace is an unstoppable trend, and because businesses are created for profitability purposes, we devote a separate chapter to the interaction between spirituality at work and the bottom line.

We will review three cases of business organizations that have done well for decades while performing spiritually, in the hope that these examples will contribute to the conviction that workplace spirituality and profitability are not only directly related but complementary phenomena.

## Spiritual Leadership and the Bottom Line

An organization achieves its highest level of performance if a spiritual mindset is established and maintained among its employees. One of the executives we interviewed in our 2003 study shared the following with us: "When you employ spirituality and leave room for discussing it, you can far exceed the normal business profit and return parameters that are occurring under the current way of doing business. I think that, by using the process of spirituality and beginning to enhance creativity and innovativeness, and taking people to different levels, the end result can be far better returns than what we have today because we're multiplying productivity so much."

> When you employ spirituality and leave room for discussing it, you can far exceed the normal business profit and return parameters that are occurring under the current way of doing business

The statement above reflects the perspective of Stephen Byrum of the Spiritual Leadership Institute. Byrum claimed, "When you create an environment where people's beliefs are respected and they are encouraged to be the best human beings they can be, then it can have a positive impact on your bottom line."(65)

Robert Giacalone and Carole Jurkiewicz also agreed with this perspective in their assertion that organizations high in workplace spirituality outperform those without it by 86 percent, and that "such organizations reportedly grow faster, increase efficiencies, and produce higher returns on investments."(66)

> *Spirituality in the workplace creates a new organizational culture in which employees feel happier and perform better.*
>
> Jean-Claude Garcia-Zamor

Jean-Claude Garcia-Zamor worded a similar conclusion in the following way: "There has been ample empirical evidence that spirituality in the workplace creates a new organizational culture in which employees feel happier and perform better." Garcia-Zamor continued, "Bringing together the motivation for work and the meaning in work increase retention. Employees also may feel that belonging to a work community, which is an important aspect of spirituality, will help them when things get rough in the future." This author emphasized that a "culture of sharing and caring eventually will reach all of the organization's stakeholders: suppliers, customers, and shareholders. In such a humanistic work environment, employees are more creative and have higher morale, two factors that are closely linked to good organizational performance."(67) Garcia-Zamor's points apply well to our previous chapter on organizational resilience, as well as to our current discussion on the bottom line. The statements from this author demonstrate the close interaction between an organization's culture and its performance, which is translated in output and, hence, profits.

## Spirituality and Profitability

How does spirituality in the workplace relate to the bottom line of a business? We will review this in more detail. Recently some publications and studies such as those cited above have focused on the relationship between workplace spirituality and organizational performance.(68) Earlier studies have shown a strong correlation between corporate culture/core values and profitability.(69) Garcia-Zamor cited a Harvard Business School study that examined 10 companies with strong corporate culture and 10 with weak corporate culture. Researchers in this study not only found a strong correlation between an organization's spirited culture and its profitability, but also found that, in some cases, the more spirited companies outperformed the others 4 to 5 times in terms of net earnings, return on investment, and shareholder value.(70)

In a 2004 article titled "The Bottom Line of Leaderful Practice," Joseph Raelin discussed the findings of a recent Gallup survey, concluding that "the most 'engaged' workplaces (those that involved people in doing quality work, fulfilling their talent, demonstrating compassion and commitment to employees' growth), compared with the least engaged, were 50 percent more likely to have lower turnover, 56 percent more likely to have higher-than-average customer loyalty, 38 percent more likely to have above-average productivity, and 27 percent more likely to report higher profitability."(71)

Corinne McLaughlin strongly emphasized the relationship between spirituality and profitability by asserting that a "growing movement across the country is promoting spiritual values in the workplace and pointing to many examples of increased productivity and profitability." This author demonstrated that many business people are finding that instituting the value of "doing well by doing good" can strengthen the bottom line. She subsequently posted the following enlightened statement:

> *A growing movement across the country is promoting spiritual values in the workplace and pointing to many examples of increased productivity and profitability.*
>
> Corinne McLaughlin

When employees are encouraged to express their creativity, the result is a more fulfilled and sustained workforce. Happy people work harder and are more likely to stay at their jobs. A study of business performance by the highly respected Wilson Learning Company found that 39 percent of the variability in corporate performance is attributable to the personal satisfaction of the staff.

According to McLaughlin, organizations that want to survive in the 21st century will have to offer a greater sense of meaning and purpose to their workforce. She emphasized that, in today's highly competitive environment, the best talent seeks out organizations that reflect their inner values and provide opportunities for personal development and community service, not just bigger salaries. McLaughlin further explained that the use of spiritual values as guiding principles has many positive effects on business. She further provided the following data linking spirituality with financial performance:

*Business Week* reported that 95 percent of Americans reject the idea that a corporation's only purpose is to make money. A recent study in Management Accounting found that companies committed to ethical business practices do better financially and have significantly greater representation among the top 100 financial performers than companies that don't make ethics a key management component. 39 percent of U.S. investors say they always or frequently check on business practices, values, and ethics before investing. The Trends Report of 1997 reported that 3 out of 4 consumers polled say they are likely to switch to brands associated with a good cause if price and quality are equal.(72)

In his explanation about how spirituality can be key to business success, William Guillory stated that the relationship between spirituality and profitability or success is based on two assumptions: 1) Profitability is a result of excellence in business function; and 2) A team of self-motivated, aligned, and high-performing individuals is the best source of sustainability and excellence."(73)

> *Spirituality in the workplace puts greater emphasis on the needs of the individual and can improve profitability because valued employees become more productive.*
>
> Dermot Tredget

In an article with the interesting title "Spirituality goes to work," Emma Clark provided an in-depth review of the many advantages of spirituality in the workplace. Clark specifically emphasized the profitability issue in the example of Father Dermot Tredget, a monk who previously held senior management positions in the corporate world. Tredget reaffirmed the claim that spirituality in the workplace puts greater emphasis on the needs of the individual and can improve profitability because valued employees become more productive."(74)

### Some Cases of Spiritual Organizations with Great Performance

### Southwest Airlines

A case study by Milliman, Ferguson, Trickett & Condemi definitively demonstrates a credible correlation between a spiritual approach and corporate profitability. They selected Southwest Airlines

> because it appears to have a strong sense of spiritual-based values guiding its organizational goals and practices. In addition, the company has an established track record of excellent organizational performance as well as high employee and customer satisfaction. In profiling SWA we certainly do not want to imply that it is a perfect example of living spiritual values; it has its problems and limitations like other firms. Despite this, there seems to be a genuine sense of spirit and affection in both SWA employees and customers.

The authors explained why they perceived SWA as a company with a highly spiritual approach, citing the organization's strong emphasis on community, teamwork, serving others, acting in the best interest of the company, employee connectedness and customer care, and an overall organizational awareness of serving an important purpose.

Milliman and his associates further claimed that SWA's core values and its implementation of those values through human resource management practices appear to generate strong employee, customer, and firm results. SWA has consistently been named in the list of 100 best companies to work for in the USA. The authors also found that, as a result of this high employee satisfaction, SWA employees have one of the lowest turnover rates (6 percent) in the airline industry. They explained:

> At the same time SWA consistently has one of the lowest labor cost per miles flown of any major airline and its employees are credited with being primarily responsible for SWA's various quality awards. Employees are also actively involved in community-based service projects. In addition, they demonstrated their support for each other by setting up a catastrophe fund to support employees during personal crises.

Milliman et. al. emphasized in their findings that many researchers feel that high employee satisfaction and productivity play a major role in SWA's profitability.(75) Subsequently elaborating on the many performance awards SWA earned in the 1990s, Milliman and associates concluded that SWA has been profitable in every year except one since it began in 1971, despite the high volatility of the airline industry. Indeed, one year in the early 1990s Southwest was the only major US airline to make a profit. And the company was able to accomplish this while maintaining strong growth. Even though SWA places a strong emphasis on customers, it underscores that its employees always come first. SWA seems to function like a big family: not only are employees encouraged to be part of the company, their families are often included in company activities and celebrations.(76).

> Even though SWA places a strong emphasis on customers, it underscores that its employees always come first.
>
> Milliman et.al

## Tom's of Maine

Another case of a company that strives to live by spiritual values is Tom's of Maine. For more than 30 years this company has created care products using pure and simple ingredients from nature. Tom Chappell, the company's Co-Founder, President, and CEO, espouses the

81

philosophy of "doing well by doing good." He started the company nearly 30 years ago with a $5,000 loan, and now it is worth more than $25 million. Chappell believes that companies should be accountable not to shareholders first, but to employees, customers, and the environment.(77) In his latest book, Chappell outlines his seven-step program (the "Seven Intentions") designed to help business managers focus on social and environmental responsibility rather than on the bottom line(78).

Tom's of Maine practices what it preaches, giving grants to various organizations and encouraging employees to spend 5 percent of their paid work time volunteering in community jobs and services. Chappell lives by the philosophy that "when companies heed 'the spirit,' the bottom line will take care of itself!" His mantra: "You don't have to sell your soul to make your numbers." On its Web site, the company makes it very clear that even if sales have grown impressively since its founding in 1970, the family orientation has endured: "This is still the kind of place where people know each other, where you notice the new faces in the crowd and can take a moment to welcome them to the community.

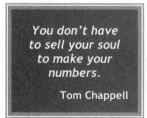

*You don't have to sell your soul to make your numbers.*

Tom Chappell

As of this writing Tom's of Maine has been acquired by Colgate-Palmolive Company. We can only hope that Colgate-Palmolive will continue the same values of sustainability and environmental friendliness that Tom's of Maine stood for.

### Herman Miller

The final case of profitability in a spiritually led company presented in this chapter is Herman Miller Furniture. In their presentation of successful business executives who demonstrate a spirituality that inspires good moral habits, Gerald Cavanagh and Mark Bandsuch reviewed Herman Miller's performance under the leadership of Max DePree. They found that, when DePree was CEO of Herman Miller, the company became very successful financially and one of the best firms in America to work for. According to Cavanagh and Bandsuch, DePree's leadership style was influenced by his spirituality. The authors concluded that DePree was convinced that his humanistic concepts had a positive effect on the organization's overall performance through its influence on the employees.

Cavanagh and Bandsuch further explain:

> DePree sees himself and other corporate leaders in a "covenantal relationship" with their people. A covenant is more than a contract: Covenantal relationships fill deep needs, enable work to have meaning and to be fulfilling. They make possible relationships that can manage conflict and change. True covenants, however, are risky because they require us to be abandoned to the talents and skills of others, and therefore to be vulnerable. The same risks that one has in falling in love.(79)

One of the ways to measure Herman Miller's successful performance is by the frequency with which the company is mentioned by a wide variety of authors on the topic of management excellence and outstanding organizational behavior. A good example is Nancy Chambers, who, in her article "The Really Long View," listed three characteristics that help a corporation last longer than the average 40 years. "They must be innovative, lean, and they have to be learning environments," she said. "My guesses for 2100 are companies like Intel, W.L. Gore & Associates, Herman Miller—and I may be running out of companies after that."(80)

Nada Korac-Kakabadse, Alexander Kouzmin, and Andrew Kakabadse(81) and Cavanagh(82) presented another important validation of Herman Miller's successful performance. They referred to the firm's regular appearance on *Fortune's* list of best-managed and most innovative companies.

> *Corporations that last are innovative, lean, and learning environments.*
>
> Nancy Chambers

Another article mentioning DePree's receipt of the 1997 Business Enterprise Award for Lifetime Achievement discussed the CEO's strategy for making Herman Miller the success story it has become. Some of DePree's extraordinary contributions to the company were:

- Helping to create a thriving work environment centered on a respect for the skills and contributions of every employee;

- Building on a foundation of participatory management by replacing traditional hierarchy with work teams;

- Adapting the Scanlon Plan, which enables employees to earn a share of productivity gains based on their suggestions;

- Introducing a profit-sharing program that rewards employees with company stock;

- • Sharing detailed financial and market information with all employees at monthly meetings, and discussing and nurturing the company's competitive edge in the industry.(83)

For those readers interested in the performance of post-DePree's Herman Miller, Peter Koudal and Todd Lavieri report that the company continues to excel. Their findings: "Herman Miller managed to grow, with gross margins increasing to 31.8% at the end of 2002, from 30.1% in 2001. Customer satisfaction grew as well. At the same time, average on-time shipping increased to 98%."(84)

## In Review

As should be clear from the foregoing examples of top performing business organizations, the application of a spiritual mindset in the workplace is not an ethereal issue by any means, but rather has immediate and remarkable effects on the organization's profits, while minimizing employee turnover and maximizing employee satisfaction.

> *Prioritizing connectivity and the people aspect will automatically lead to enhanced organizational performance.*

The companies reviewed in this chapter all perform toward strengthening their bottom line. But they have one additional thing in common: they prioritize connectivity and the people aspect, realizing that these acts will automatically lead to enhanced organizational performance. And this is also the single point that makes them stand out when compared to organizations that refrain from nurturing relationships. While shortsighted entities may enjoy a short increase in performance, they begin a predictable descent as soon as turnover and costs for training new employees increase as a result of a dissatisfied workforce.

## Reflection Sheet

These areas represent the contents of this chapter that I consider applicable to my life:

_____
_____
_____
_____
_____
_____
_____
_____

These areas represent the contents of this chapter whose applicability to my life I question:

_____
_____
_____
_____
_____
_____
_____
_____
_____
_____

My personal opinions after reading this chapter:

_____
_____
_____
_____
_____
_____

What I would like to remember:

_____
_____
_____
_____
_____
_____
_____

# Chapter 7

## Accomplishing Connectivity

In this chapter we will present an integral model of spirituality in the workplace and comment on the various factors involved in this model.

The model will serve as a step-by-step explanation of spirituality in the workplace in action, thereby also bringing into view the emergent paradigm reviewed in above chapters—workplace spirituality as manifested in employee fulfillment and workplace performance. We will evaluate how the various dimensions of the model tie into each other, and so create the positive cycle that is generated by a spiritual workplace.

## Formulation of a Broadly Acceptable Definition

As a result of our research in recent years, we formulated a definition of spirituality in the workplace. The definition, which we already presented in chapters 1 and 5, was formulated around one paradigm, which may be profiled as follows:

> A hundred times every day I remind myself that my inner and outer life depend on the labors of other men, living and dead, and that I must exert myself in order to give in the same measure as I have received and am still receiving.
>
> Albert Einstein

1. A person should connect with the source within;
2. This inner-connection will enhance interconnectedness with others;
3. Interconnectedness leads to a better work environment;
4. A better internal work environment improves the overall organizational performance externally.

## The Definition and the Model

Once again we will revisit the definition of spirituality in the workplace as we have formulated it in above chapters:

> *Spirituality in the workplace is an experience of interconnectedness among those involved in a work process; initiated by authenticity, reciprocity, and personal goodwill; engendered by a deep sense of meaning that is inherent in the organization's work; and resulting in greater motivation and organizational excellence.*

Figure 7.1 on the next page represents the findings of our research and a subsequent analysis of the points captured. As the model demonstrates, spirituality in the workplace requires the following:

1. A set of personal (internal) factors within each individual who wants to operate at his or her highest level of spiritual awareness;
2. A set of integrated qualities that this person will apply in his or her connection with other spiritual workers;
3. A set of externally applicable factors that this person needs to maintain with others in his or her environment. These factors should correspond with the internal factors of the organization;
4. A set of factors that the organization as an entity should integrate, maintain, and apply internally;
5. A set of factors that the organization as an entity should apply externally;
6. A set of consequential experiences that should flow back to the spiritual worker.

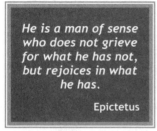

*He is a man of sense who does not grieve for what he has not, but rejoices in what he has.*

Epictetus

### Individual-Internal Factors
For each individual in the workplace, starting with top management and moving down to all levels of employees, the following qualities should be encouraged: honesty, creativeness, productivity, kindness, dependability, confidence, and courage.

### Individual-Integrated Factors
As the model demonstrates, there is a set of integrated themes at work between the individual and his or her work environment. Through interconnectedness with similar-minded individuals (colleagues, supervisors, and subordinates), a positive organizational culture is created. This culture will be characterized by an aesthetically pleasing environment, consisting of a set of factors that can be seen as the external environment for the individual as well as the internal environment for the organization (see specification below).

### Individual-External Factors/Organizational-Internal Factors
The above mentioned external factors for the individual and internal factors for the organization include a sense of purpose, high ethical standards, acceptance, peace, trust, respect, understanding, appreciation, care, involvement, helpfulness, encouragement, achievement, and perspective.

### Organizational-Integrated Factors
The factors presented above lead to integrated organizational factors such as enhanced team performance and harmony.

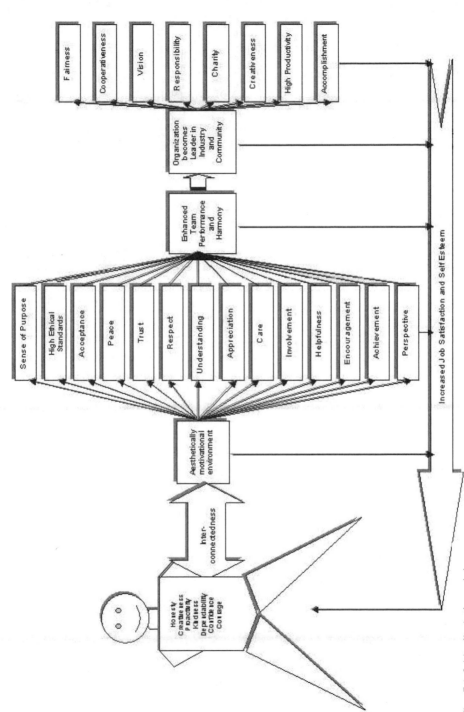

Figure 7.1: Spirituality in the workplace

The integrated organizational factors further result in improved organizational performance, which will increase the company's competitive advantage and enable a number of positive external characteristics for the organization.

### Organizational-External Factors

Some of the external characteristics of an organization with the above-described culture are (as our research findings point out) fairness, cooperativeness, vision, responsibility, charity, creativeness, high productivity, and accomplishments.

## Discussion of the Themes

### Individual Internal

Honesty: An individual with an honest approach makes a better impression on his or her surroundings. Honesty is contagious. When people in a workplace know that their leaders are open and truthful in their information sharing, they are encouraged to do the same.

> *Where is there dignity unless there is honesty?*
>
> Cicero

Creativeness: Every workplace continuously faces circumstances that require creativity in finding solutions. If employees are encouraged to try new things, to share their ideas, and to apply their insights in their daily tasks, the results for the organization overall can only be positive.

Productivity: An employee who feels accepted and recognized, and who enjoys regular training, mentoring, and coaching to keep his or her skills up to par, does everything in his or her power to increase productivity.

Kindness: This may be perceived as the most contagious theme in the entire spectrum. A leader who is kind toward his or her subordinates usually earns a similar response; an organization where kind people work is one where everyone likes to be.

Dependability: An employee who can be counted on also sends out a positive message into the workplace and often receives a similar approach in return from colleagues.

Confidence: A person who believes in him- or herself dares to apply more personal input in the workplace, offer more suggestions, participate in more company activities, and affect others in this positive environment with the same approach.

Courage: This characteristic can be seen as an extension to confidence, and also as a quality to thrive during times of change and uncertainty.

## Individual Integrated

Interconnectedness: If all employees in a workplace have most of the above-mentioned individual mentalities, there is a high sense of recognition in each other, and thus, interconnectedness. A family-style atmosphere and a "we" spirit is thereby established.

## Individual External-Organizational Internal

Aesthetically pleasing environment: Employees with a high sense of interconnectedness try to make the workplace, where they spend more than one-third of their life, as pleasant as can be. It is not strange when people bring in plants, pictures, affirmations, and other pleasantries from home to enhance the atmosphere at work.

Sense of purpose: A tone of honesty, openness, and dependability provides for a free flow of information and a high level of access to employees at all levels. If the goals and strategies are clearly and regularly communicated throughout the company, there is an increased sense of purpose among the employees.

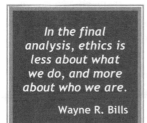

*In the final analysis, ethics is less about what we do, and more about who we are.*

Wayne R. Bills

High ethical standards: Top management should model this trait throughout the organization. Ethics cannot merely be taught or mentioned, but has to be lived in order to take effect. Ethical approaches start with top management and trickle down throughout the organization.

Acceptance: A company with a culture of acceptance among all employees, regardless of backgrounds, race, ethnicity, age, gender, education, position, or appearance, establishes a strong bond: one team where everyone is part of the in-crowd, everyone belongs, and everyone is encouraged to perform.

Peace: This theme may be more sensible than visible in a workplace where people communicate with each other in a friendly manner, and where the overall atmosphere radiates warmth and hospitality.

Trust: In a company culture where people believe in honesty and dependability and where acceptance is a given, there is no backstabbing and no inappropriate company politics. As a result there is trust, without cause to posture or prevaricate.

Respect: The workplace that practices acceptance among employees also practices respect for them and for all others who regularly or incidentally interact with the company.

Understanding: Because there is so much openness and warmth among employees, there is an increased willingness to understand each other.

Appreciation: In a work environment with a spiritual culture, people appreciate each other and those they serve.

Care: This theme pertains to the concern one individual displays toward another who experiences difficulties in certain areas: there is no harshness; there is empathy and team spirit in trying to help this colleague to feel better.

Involvement: This element is yet another result of an organizational culture with a free information flow and high accessibility levels in which employees feel increasingly involved and display a greater willingness to perform better.

Helpfulness: Not only within one department, but between departments, as well as between employees and third parties (suppliers, customers, the community), a sense of cooperation and goodwill pervades.

Encouragement: This theme can be placed in the same category as acceptance, care, and helpfulness: employees contributing to a spiritual work environment encourage each other, as well as all parties they deal with, in times of need.

> I believe that any man's life will be filled with constant and unexpected encouragement, if he makes up his mind to do his level best each day, and as nearly as possible reaching the high water mark of pure and useful living.
>
> Booker T. Washington

Achievement: If there is team spirit, understanding, acceptance, helpfulness, kindness, and openness, and if it can be assumed that top management does not withhold the necessary training and materials toward production, achievement is a logical consequence.

Perspective: Employees who are aware of the company's goals and strategies are well aware of their importance to the organization, and will subsequently develop their own viewpoint on production processes and overall performance issues, which they share with colleagues and managers.

**Organizational Integrated**
Enhanced team performance: All the themes mentioned in the segment above contribute to the establishment of great team spirit throughout the organization, and, thus, enhanced team performance.

Harmony: Where teams are regularly in process, especially if they are cross-functional, there is more understanding and respect for one another's jobs, and there is more harmony in interactions and production flows.

**Organizational External**
Competitive advantage: A company where the themes discussed above are in place simply perform better than those that have rigid hierarchical structures. The company with an open and sensitive culture enjoys a clear competitive advantage due to greater team performance and communication.

> Though force can protect in emergency, only justice, fairness, consideration and co-operation can finally lead men to the dawn of eternal peace.
>
> Dwight D. Eisenhower

Fairness: Although most companies are in business for profit, the one with the above-described organizational culture applies fairness in its encounters with all stakeholders, including competitors.

Cooperativeness: This is a very important theme. An organization that enables a cooperative culture is far more adaptive than one with a hostile environment.

Vision: Due to the great interaction within a spiritually inclined organization and between the company and its stakeholders, a vision emerges that leads this company to greater heights than initially anticipated, because there is a spirit of sharing instead of withholding.

Responsibility: A company with this culture is highly involved in community development and takes responsibility for its actions. This also entails, for instance, that the company will not engage in deliberate and negligent environmental damage.

Charity: This company's high community involvement is expressed through charity toward individuals and environmental issues.

Creativeness: While this trait was already mentioned as an individual skill, it recurs here as a skill that the organization radiates in its performance. Problems are solved in a proactive way, while new ideas emerge and are executed at a higher pace and with greater success than competitors.

High productivity: This is the logical consequence of a close connection among employees, between employees and top management, and between company representatives and stakeholders.

Accomplishments: High productivity is but one of the accomplishments of this type of organization. Far more important in the interconnectedness are high job satisfaction for employees, positive interaction with stakeholders, and the company's overall reputation as a good citizen.

The above statements all illustrate how the participants in our studies perceived the structural meaning of connectivity in a workplace that nurtures the spiritual mindset. The essence of the above-presented statements can be summarized in the following statement: An employee can only perform at his or her highest level of spiritual awareness, and consequently help create a workplace that nurtures this mindset, if he or she can connect to his or her deepest inner values (that is, realizes that he or she is a spiritual being), which enhances the connection with other individuals in the workplace, ultimately creating a more pleasant work environment.

> As human beings, our greatness lies not so much in being able to remake the world—that is the myth of the atomic age—as in being able to remake ourselves.
>
> Mahatma Gandhi

We found that there are various essential meanings to be formulated when comparing the above-mentioned findings with other literature on the topic and our own work experiences. We therefore limited ourselves to the following essentials of workplace spirituality, based on our studies, on literature reviewed, and on our personal experiences:

1. Working with a spiritual mindset ultimately results in higher productivity and better organizational performance.
2. People who feel that they are understood put in the reciprocal effort to understand. This process creates goodwill and a sense of connection, and brings people in alignment with each other.
3. People regularly involved in processes and decisions in their workplace tend to see the bigger picture of what they are doing, and therefore obtain a larger level of satisfaction at their job, which also positively influences their level of self-esteem.
4. When people are aware of each others' unique perspectives and contribution capacities, they respect each other more and perceive their differences as useful, which leads to better team

performance and, hence, richer outcomes for the organization as well as the individuals involved.

5. If leadership in an organization nurtures the spiritual mindset, then the chance of successful establishment of this phenomenon is almost guaranteed.

## In Review

An additional presentation of statements by various study participants about their deepest convictions could enlighten readers regarding the right attitude in the workplace and the actual implementation of the spiritual mindset. These statements could also serve as an effective summary of what was discussed in this chapter. Listed below are the statements:

1. Spirituality in the workplace requires belief in one's self and in positive outcomes, even when times are grim.

*Spirituality in the workplace starts with the acknowledgement that every entity, individual, or group has a spirit.*

2. Spirituality in the workplace is encouraged when the people who work in that environment take good care of themselves in every regard: mentally, physically, and spiritually.

3. Spirituality in the workplace starts with the acknowledgement that every entity, individual, or group has a spirit.

4. Spirituality in the workplace does not only result in good outcomes within one's own work environment, but ultimately in a better performing organization, and therefore a better society.

5. Spirituality is not religion, but rather the connection with one's deepest inner self. Spirituality in the workplace, therefore, has nothing to do with the enforcement of religion at work.

6. The cultivation of a spiritual mindset ideally starts early in life, preferably at home or in school, so that more people can enter the work environment with a positive outlook on life and exude this outlook toward their co-workers.

7. Spirituality in the workplace is based on interconnectedness. However, this factor should not just be established among the employees who are performing at their highest spiritual awareness; instead, it should be maintained through the creation of an environment within the organization where all employees are

encouraged to talk about and learn from it. This is an excellent way to expand the spiritual mindset.

8. Spirituality in the workplace is not necessarily an ethereal phenomenon, and in no way should it lead to decreased performance in business settings. On the contrary, applying a spiritual mindset in the workplace encourages creativity and innovativeness within the employees, which enhances their productivity and leads to a better overall performance of the organization.

9. The application of spirituality in the workplace should not be underestimated for future global developments. Since it is questionable whether governments or non-profit organizations can be capable of properly handling worldwide environmental, health care,

> *The application of spirituality in the workplace should not be underestimated for future global developments. It will be up to the business environment to enhance global progress and interconnectedness.*

aging, and security issues in every case, the private sector should attempt to provide solutions as well. The business environment should thus implement a more empathetic approach in its performance. This empathetic approach starts with the people factor in every working organization. When people are treated well and feel that they truly matter, they increase their output and put forth greater effort to improve the national, regional, and global position of their workplace. Once this position of work environments that nurture the spiritual mindset is established, the betterment of the societies in which these organizations operate should follow.

Fortunately, spirituality in the workplace is gradually rising above its unearthly interpretation and is starting to become a better-understood phenomenon, although it is still not generally referred to as such. Many organizations, especially the ones performing in strict and high-paced settings such as the business environment, prefer to express the concept of spirituality as quality of life, business renaissance, or simply corporate social responsibility programs. Yet, in many ways these programs are prompted by the spiritual process displayed in this chapter.

Once again we should emphasize that our studies demonstrate that spirituality in the workplace has little to do with religion, but everything to do with interconnectedness. Like some of the participants in our studies asserted, the awareness of being interconnected reaches much further than merely in the workplace—it affects other environments of the employee who performs at his or her highest level of spiritual awareness, at home and in all possible social settings. More effectively, such awareness benefits the organizational network and the interaction between organizations and communities. If it appears to be a far-fetched vision, it is not as improbable as one might think.

> *Spirituality in the workplace has little to do with religion, but everything to do with interconnectedness. The awareness of being interconnected reaches much further than merely in the workplace—it affects the individual worker, the organizational network, and the interaction between organizations and communities.*

## Reflection Sheet

These areas represent the contents of this chapter that I consider applicable to my life:

These areas represent the contents of this chapter whose applicability to my life I question:

My personal opinions after reading this chapter:

What I would like to remember:

# Part III

## Spirituality in the Workplace: How To Make it Work for You

### Internal and External Dimensions

# Chapter 8

## Personal Contributions Toward a Spiritual Workplace

Being a spiritual worker is sometimes a natural way of performing, but it can also be an evolving process, triggered by experiences. In this chapter we will review possible reasons for a person to become a spiritual worker. We will then assess some characteristics of a spiritual worker and some actions spiritual workers could undertake to enhance the level of spirituality in their workplace.

## Transforming into a Spiritual Worker

When looking at workplaces in general, one wonders why some people have a higher tendency to cooperate and be helpful than others. Once you are aware of this difference in employees' behavior, an interesting question emerges: How could somebody transform from an employee who does not attempt to live and work with spiritual values and practices to one who does?

> Be the change you want to see in the world.
>
> Mahatma Gandhi

When we asked students and members of the workforce this question during the past years, most of them concluded that the primary motive for someone to change from an overly individualistic, over-protective, and non-cooperative employee into a more spiritually oriented person would be a radically life-altering experience. And this idea makes sense. When someone is confronted with severe illness or some other life-changing experience such as marriage, the birth of a child, the death of a loved one, or even a dramatic occurrence in his or her career, the person tends to reevaluate his or her perspectives. It is often due to the affection and attention experienced from unexpected sources that this person will start realizing the flaws in his or her prior behavior. But there could be more reasons that people change from inconsiderate and selfish to more sensitive and spiritually attuned. Below is a list of reasons we collected from our multiple readings, interviews, and personal observations in this regard. People can positively change into more spiritually attuned employees due to:

- Confrontation with a life-changing event: accident, birth of a child, marriage, death of a loved one, or any other traumatic experience;
- Influences from spiritually engaged leaders or spiritually engaged colleagues in the workplace;

105

- Influences from spiritually engaged thinkers outside of the workplace, whose impact reaches all areas of the affected person's life;
- Dealing with excessive stress: When confronted with tremendous personal or work-related stress, a person can decide that the mental pressure needs to be relieved. This can cause the employee to exit a harsh work environment in which he or she used to get along fairly well before, and opt for a more spiritually attuned workplace;
- A growing aversion toward ruthless external or internal workplace competition, which can also lead to a search for a more spiritually attuned workplace;
- A desire to be part of an organization that has demonstrated excellence through the application of spirituality in the workplace: this may also lead an individual to decide toward engagement into the practice of a more spiritual mindset;

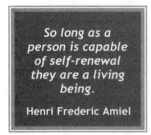

So long as a person is capable of self-renewal they are a living being.

Henri Frederic Amiel

- A desire to make a positive difference and lead by example, not just in the workplace, but also outside of work. This sense may emerge when a person takes on new responsibilities, either at work or in the private areas of his or her life—a management position, marriage, or a family.

As we categorize some of the catalysts that spur people on to become more spiritually attuned, we see two clusters emerge: 1) internally inspired; and 2) externally driven. These clusters provide further insight into the transformations described above:

1. **Internally inspired transformation**: The list below presents personal changes that can cause an employee to become more spiritually attuned, even when not working in a spiritually sound environment. Still, the employee's shift in perspective could lead to his or her spiritual influence on the work environment. Some specific internal catalysts that can transform an employee include

   ✓ A raised level of consciousness;
   ✓ A confrontation with a life-changing problem;
   ✓ A change of habits;
   ✓ A change of lifestyle (for instance, getting married or starting to raise children and therefore wanting to lead by example);
   ✓ A general desire for inner peace and self-satisfaction;
   ✓ A developed aversion to a competitive environment;

    ✓  A newly obtained will to feel better about one's self, work, colleagues, and society;

    ✓  An aversion toward a heavy-handed hierarchical structure.

2.  **Externally driven transformation:** In this case, the company culture encourages the employee to adapt to a broader spiritual mindset in order to perform well in a socially oriented setting. External catalysts of this nature include:

    ✓  A response to positive influences from colleagues;

    ✓  A receptivity to new ideas and a new way of thinking;

    ✓  The will to be involved in a successful, inventive organization.

Table 8.1 presents the above overview in a more structured manner.

Table 8.1. Events that can transform a non-spiritual worker into a spiritual worker.

| Internally inspired: | Externally driven: |
|---|---|
| • A personal change that can cause the employee to become spiritual without working in a spiritual environment<br>• A raised level of consciousness<br>• Confrontation with a life-changing problem<br>• Change of habits<br>• Change of lifestyle (getting married and starting to raise children—a desire to lead by example)<br>• Desire for inner peace and self-satisfaction<br>• Aversion to a competitive environment<br>• The will to feel better about one's self, work, colleagues, and society<br>• Aversion to a heavy-handed hierarchical structure | • The result of a converted company culture<br>• The positive influences of others<br>• The will to be involved in a groundbreaking organization<br>• Openness to new ideas and a new way of thinking |

### Behavior of a spiritual worker

Another interesting list of behavior and guidelines for readers who may want to evaluate their own workplace behavior emerges when we ask the following questions:

- What do spiritual workers do?
- What do spiritual workers refrain from doing?

Table 8.2 lists phrases that corporate workers, leaders, and students of business and management mentioned in regard to what spiritual workers actually do and don't do. To continue the trend we started above, we compile three categories of behavior: 1) internal; 2) integrated (toward other individuals); and 3) external (toward groups).

Table 8.2. Most frequently used phrases regarding what a spiritual worker would do and would NOT do.

| What a spiritual worker will do | What a spiritual worker will NOT do |
|---|---|
| **Internally** ||
| Motivate | Be negative |
| Be honest | Be dishonest |
| Be open | |
| Achieve | |
| Commit | |
| Be receptive | |
| Be creative | |
| Seek truth | |
| **Integrated** ||
| Be understanding | Be selfish |
| Have respect | |
| Listen | |
| **Externally** ||
| Give | Engage in crass politics |
| Pursue quality | |
| Mentor | |
| Be fair | |
| Encourage | |
| Be creative | |

In Chapter 7, where we presented an integrated model for spirituality in the workplace, we brought a number of these and other behaviors into an entire organizational picture, each with a brief explanation of its contents and meaning. We now review Figure 7.1 from the individual perspective as discussed in this chapter.

## Enhancing the Level of Spirituality in the Workplace

### Maintaining flexibility

As we mentioned at the beginning of this chapter, there are various reasons at the foundation of people's need to seek a more spiritual work environment. Some of these reasons were, as you may recall, a growing aversion to the stress and competition that some workplaces present, and the fact that many people, once they mature and raise children themselves, desire to lead by example and thus want to display a more spiritual mentality in all areas of their lives.

Especially for the more mature workers, the aspiration to participate in a more spiritual work environment derives from changes in life perceptions: growing experience, increased moderation, increased compliance, and more receptiveness, to name a few. In colloquial terms one might say, "The sharp edges fade and the relativity of things becomes apparent."

In a spiritual workplace employees learn to accept their colleagues, supervisors, subordinates, and customers for what they are worth. They learn to respect their points of view no matter how radically these may oppose theirs. As spiritual workers, they realize that, although spirituality does not have to mean agreeing with everything and everybody, it *does* entail valuing the fact that others may have different perceptions about certain issues. Spiritual workers realize that the divergent viewpoints of others around them do not have to form an obstacle in the creation of a pleasant and productive work environment—quite the contrary! Different perspectives can enrich the spiritual worker's awareness if he or she cares to listen, and they can help this employee determine whether his or her old points of view are still acceptable within his or her matured state of mind, or whether these views need to be revised. More importantly, the spiritual worker knows that an empathetic attitude at work creates a bond among colleagues that stretches beyond the boundaries of the work environment.

> An oak and a reed were arguing about their strength. When a strong wind came up, the reed avoided being uprooted by bending and leaning with the gusts of wind. But the oak stood firm and was torn up by the roots.
>
> Aesop

Spiritual workers are also aware that there will always be people who do not respond to a positive attitude, no matter how hard they try. That may have to do with branding—these individuals may have decided from the very start that they would not like certain co-workers, regardless of how nice they are or how well they perform. Branding is an unfortunate trait that is primarily created in the environment in which one grows up and is nurtured by the mindsets of the people in that environment. When people brand others based on outward appearances—stereotyping—they degrade themselves into ignorant souls, unwilling to accept others and grow. With those unwilling souls, the spiritual worker should not do much more than remain correct in his or her approach toward them, while protecting his or her dignity by not giving away too much of him- or herself. This behavior could be referred to as *healthy detachment*.

This simple theory forms the basis for establishing spirituality at work: respecting and accepting others for who or what they are, and remaining righteous toward those who have a clear antipathy against us.

*A label is easy to stick on, but difficult to remove.*

Unknown

Yet, a word of caution may be in order here: If the people who express an antipathy toward the spiritual worker hold powerful positions, or if they form a majority in the workplace, the spiritual worker may well consider a job change and take his or her spiritual approach elsewhere. After all, if spirituality in the workplace translates itself in one's level of job satisfaction, then workplaces populated with a majority of unwilling souls cannot offer as much. And then, the ultimate spiritual workplace may very well be the one that the spiritual worker creates from scratch, in his or her own entrepreneurial organization.

However, even if a person is not at all interested in becoming his or her own boss and workforce at the same time, this individual can still determine the level of spirituality he or she prefers at his or her workplace by modeling respect and correctness toward colleagues, or by simply changing workplaces until he or she has found the right fit.

If we are all spiritual beings with a human experience, then every workplace where people come together to perform is a spiritual one. What we have to strive for is to ensure that the degree of our workplace spirituality aligns with our personal spiritual needs. Once the match is found, the results will speak for themselves; the increase in job satisfaction will be phenomenal, and productivity will reach impressive heights.

### Applying a positive attitude

We have all probably read or heard more than once about changing situations if they do not add to our quality of life. Such encouragement can be helpful, but unfortunately it is not always applicable in the short term. Just consider the job market: We all know how grim that looks these days! Jobs are being outsourced left and right in this emerging global village, even jobs that were once considered "non-outsourceable." So, although we just mentioned the option of a job change when matters become unbearable in one workplace, the fact remains that quitting one job before finding a sufficient, satisfying, and reasonably paying alternative is not always going to be the most wise decision. Immediate exit is only responsible when a person has saved a decent sum of money to maintain his or her needs and those of his or her dependents during the time that he or she screens the classifieds in the newspaper or on the Internet. The more responsibility one has, the less likely it is for him or her to leap out of the current work environment into an unknown that may contain every possible surprise.

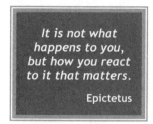

*It is not what happens to you, but how you react to it that matters.*

Epictetus

Yet there is hope for a spiritual worker. It is called *attitude*. Epictetus, a Roman slave of Greek origin, who later came to be recognized as a great Stoic thinker, figured it out many centuries ago, and wise people have quoted his words in several settings since: "It is not what happens to you, but how you react to it that matters."(85) This, then, is the unification of two phenomena that can elevate the quality of one's life significantly. It confronts a given, one's current situation, with the only tool one has to make it better—one's attitude.

In their book *Fish! Tales*, Stephen Lundin, John Christensen, and Harry Paul emphasized this very issue in a striking, warmhearted way: a woman is assigned the immense task of turning around a poorly performing department, up till then infamous throughout the organization for its unproductive and toxic work atmosphere. She ultimately finds the solution at a fish market, where the fishmongers display a contagiously upbeat attitude by humorously entertaining their customers, communicating with them in a direct and caring manner, and encouraging them to share in their fun and excitement, all while selling something as smelly and ordinary as fish. The message becomes clear to the woman when she gets a few friendly hints and tips from the manager of the fish market. The message is simple: "If you have to do it anyway, choose your best attitude to do it, and it will pay off." How? Well, alertness, friendliness, helpfulness, and dedication seldom remain unrecognized by customers, co-workers, or supervisors. The gratitude you receive from the most unexpected corners is a worthwhile encouragement to continue the good work.

The best thing about taking the right attitude to work is that it is contagious, like hearing someone laughing so hard you cannot help laughing too, even if you do not know what it is all about—or like seeing someone yawn and automatically starting to yawn too, even when you are not sleepy. It works like sex appeal: people catch the vibes and see you in a different light. And it is like a cool breeze on a hot day: your smile and cooperative attitude will wipe away many a frown that initially come your way.

Of course it is understandable that a person, no matter how spiritually minded, may not be able to shine with the same intensity every day, but once this person's positive approach has become known at the office and has affected his or her colleagues, their empathy will very likely not be hard to find when problems occur, and they will do everything in their power to lift the spiritual worker up when he or she needs it.

> *If you don't like something, change it. If you can't change it, change your attitude. Don't complain.*
>
> Maya Angelou

Therefore, a spiritual worker should not allow him- or herself to feel lost if he or she carries a lot of responsibilities and cannot physically change the status quo right away. There is still one condition that a spiritual worker can always determine—one major choice: *the choice of one's personal approach, or attitude*.

The greatest impact this positive approach can have is that it can exceed the boundaries of one's department and catch the attention of other divisions in the workplace, or even of other companies in the industry. And who knows—this positive attitude could lead to a superb job offer before too long. However, *because* of one's positive attitude, and the subsequent positive spirit activated at work, the spiritual worker may not even *want* to consider a change of work environment or employer anymore. For, in line with Mahatma Gandhi's famous statement, *"Be the change you want to see in the world,"* a positive spiral may have been created in a previously harsh work environment, and this workplace may have evolved into an utterly rewarding and fulfilling one for all of its employees.

### Incorporating a personal touch
Since one of the main goals of a spiritual worker is to obtain fulfillment through finding meaning in his or her workplace, it may be a logical consequence that this employee will exert efforts in transforming the workplace into a pleasant one. That is, a place where all stakeholders—customers, co-workers, suppliers, visitors, and shareholders—feel comfortable, uninhibited, satisfied, motivated and cared for. Yet, we also know that establishing this effect is not always the easiest thing. This is especially the case in work environments where offices are minimized to cubicles with extreme limitations to space, privacy, and movement. These maze-like settings require some kind of inventive

approach to mitigate the consequential loss of creativity, motivation, and general work spirit.

The following five suggestions may help an employee revitalize the spirit in his or her workplace or simply maintain the positive approach with which he or she stepped into this work environment.

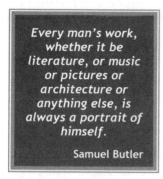

*Every man's work, whether it be literature, or music or pictures or architecture or anything else, is always a portrait of himself.*

Samuel Butler

1. Bring in some personal belongings—a picture of the kids, a painting from your son, a funny sculpture from your daughter, or your beloved Garfield desk calendar—and place them where you can often see them. The regular exposure to familiar belongings, coming from an environment where you feel contented, can help you to obtain a sense of comfort in a more stressful place.

2. Plants can help. A real plant that requires regular watering may not work well for those of us who are forgetful. And foliage the size of a mini tree might narrow your workspace even more. But small plants and flowers take up minimal space, yet enliven the space they occupy. Those are the ones to look for.

3. Take regular breaks (no matter how short) through the day to walk to a place where you can see the world outside. Some workplaces cannot provide for this human need. Staff members in these places therefore lose their sense of time entirely until the workday is over. But we should never underestimate the value of experiencing trees, people, the weather, or anything else that reminds us of the world that exists outside of the camp we spend our days in. It may be crucial for our imaginative capacities to stay in touch with these simple reminders.

4. Keep your career dreams alive. Depending on what they are, you will have to find a way to execute this process. For instance, if you want to have your own office someday, enroll in evening or weekend college courses and learn the skills required to apply for the job that will provide you a more desirable work climate. If you do not know yet what exactly it is that you want to do, just read. Magazines or online sources such as *Entrepreneur, Fortune,* and *Forbes* can trigger some positive vibes in you, stirring up your creative juices and surfacing an idea for your future direction. Keep a few of these magazines within reach at your desk.

5.  Guard your attitude. Many teachers in past centuries have emphasized the importance of attitude under the most discouraging circumstances. The concentration camp survivor Viktor Frankl and the above-mentioned teacher Epictetus are two of them. Frankl's concentration camp survival quote may be appropriate here: "Everything can be taken from a man but one thing; the last of the human freedoms—to choose one's attitude in any given set of circumstances, to choose one's own way."(86)

The perception of these survivors is that we may not always be able to decide upon our circumstances, but we do master our attitude toward them. And since the cubicle-labyrinths are such ideal hearths for transmission, you could make your healthy attitude the source of proliferation. What often helps is to post some of your favorite motivational citations there where you (and your colleagues) can often see them. "A healthy attitude is contagious, but don't wait to catch it from others. Be a carrier."(87)

> Everything can be taken from a man but one thing; the last of the human freedoms—to choose one's attitude in any given set of circumstances, to choose one's own way.
>
> Viktor E. Frankl

### Refraining from disdain

Near the end of this chapter, we would like to elaborate on a topic that is eminent in becoming and remaining a spiritual worker: refraining from disdain. Too often people have a tendency to take their own activities seriously, and regard with contempt—or simply underestimate—those of others. This attitude may not necessarily come from arrogance, but more from unawareness of the value others place in their respective activities. Yet, it can be experienced as hurtful by the ones scorned, and could even create enemies where there was no intention to do so.

The individual who has a job in which he or she works with his or her hands and body all day may look down on the activities of the one who performs his or her daily tasks—activities that may require few physical skills—in a suit and tie. The one who earns his or her daily bread as a salesperson may frown upon the satisfaction someone else obtains from being a computer technician or a receptionist. Top executives may look down on maintenance workers because they assume that these people are less educated and work in a less stressful environment without really having to use their brains, while, at the same time, maintenance workers may think in a denigrating way about those executives who sit behind their large desks, attend business luncheons, participate in conference calls and Internet meetings, lifting nothing heavier than a pen on a daily basis. Older employees who earned their positions through years of practice and life lessons may look down on young executives who obtain high positions with little or no experience beyond obtaining a college degree. At the same time, the young executives may frown upon those stubborn older supervisors who seem to oppose every radical innovation and want to continue doing things the way they have been done for the past 50 years.

Disdain is a widespread perceptional disease that is totally uncalled for if we consider the real essence of life. Every job, task, position, and level of intellect fills a need. The world would neither prosper with only educated executives nor with only physical workers, neither with only strategists nor with only line personnel, neither with only experiential nor with only theoretical knowledge. Since we all rely on each other's talents, everybody should have a sufficient level of respect for the skills of others.

> Don't be condescending to unskilled labor. Try it for a half a day first.
>
> Brooks Atkinson

The diversity reflected in the macrocosm of the universe is also mirrored in the diversity within each human being by way of uniqueness, creativity, and circumstances.

The employee who plows and sows all day may not see the actual plow or spade in the office clerk's hands, but he or she should know that the job of the office clerk is just as important to the continuation of our system; the tools may be different, but the goal is the same: survival, contributing to the progress of the system, and obtaining a sense of purpose.

It is so easy to look at the world from our own little cubicle and feel as if we are the only ones with a yoke on our shoulders, especially when we compare our lives and tasks to others'. However, we should realize that looking from the outside into other people's worlds only gives us a limited view of what is really going on there: the man who drives his ultra luxurious car to work and lives in a mansion may have many sleepless nights about decisions to be made at work, or bills to be paid; and the woman who stays at home to take care of the kids and the house may be much more stressed with her daily tasks than anyone on the outside can possibly imagine.

Disdain would probably end immediately if, by some magical act of fate, we could be placed in the shoes of those we underestimate, if only for a day. In lieu of such a circumstance, however, we must exorcise our disdain through communication and the enhancement of our awareness that everyone and everything is as valuable as we consider ourselves to be. Just as we experience our own sense of *I*—our sense of purpose and presence—others experience theirs. It is this minuscule thought that could help us decrease feelings of reciprocal disdain, and instead elevate our sense of understanding and empathy among each other, enhance our mutual respect, contribute to a greater interconnectedness, and, consequentially, a more spiritual workplace.

## Recommendations

Each individual in every workplace should realize that the creation of a pleasant work environment starts with his or her attitude. As many management authors and business executives have stated before, one needs to realize that he or she is driven by an inner source or inner power that needs to have a certain combination of characteristics in order to perform well and make the work process a rewarding experience for everyone involved.

> The best person is like water.
> Water is good; it benefits all things and does not compete with them.
> It dwells in [lowly] places that all disdain.
> This is why it is so near to Tao.
>
> Lao Tzu

People who seek to perform at their optimal spiritual awareness will first have to apply the process of inner-connection or *interbeing*, as coined by Thich Nhat Hanh, a Vietnamese monk. When one reaches inside and gets in touch with his or her determining drive—often called *soul, spirit, God, conscience,* or simply, *inner source*—the most probable elements that should emerge are honesty, creativeness, proactivity, kindness, dependability, confidence, and courage. This can be considered the set of inner traits that define a good colleague.

In order to develop these personal traits, one should focus not only on achieving a spiritual equilibrium, which can be reached in a variety of ways—meditating, performing yoga, or spending regular time in nature-rich settings—but also on establishing general mental, physical, and emotional health. Therefore, the value of seemingly simple acts such as regular physical workouts, good eating habits, and regular relaxing activities should not be underestimated.

> *Our lives as we lead them are passed on to others, whether in physical or mental forms, tingeing all future lives together. This should be enough for one who lives for truth and service to his fellow passengers on the way.*
>
> Luther Burbank

## Reflection Sheet

These areas represent the contents of this chapter that I consider applicable to my life:

_____
_____
_____
_____
_____
_____
_____

These areas represent the contents of this chapter whose applicability to my life I question:

_____
_____
_____
_____
_____
_____
_____
_____
_____

My personal opinions after reading this chapter:

_____
_____
_____
_____
_____
_____

What I would like to remember:

_____
_____
_____
_____
_____
_____
_____

# Chapter 9

## Organizational Contributions Toward a Spiritual Workplace

In this chapter we will focus further on elements of spirituality in the workplace. Subsequently, we will evaluate some of the factors that can transform a non-spiritual workplace into a spiritual one. We will also review managerial actions that are crucial in establishing such a workplace.

## Elements of a Spiritual Workplace

In our studies about workplace spirituality, we asked the participants a number of questions. These questions were all very useful in producing a list of attention points for management and policy makers in a business organization on their way to establishing and nurturing a spiritual workplace.

One of the questions we consistently asked in order to obtain an answer at the organizational level was: "If an organization is consciously attempting to nurture spirituality in the workplace, what will be present?"

> *A man is not rightly conditioned until he is a happy, healthy, and prosperous being; and happiness, health, and prosperity are the result of a harmonious adjustment of the inner with the outer of the man with his surroundings.*
>
> James Allen

From the responses of study participants, workshop attendees, and other executives we interviewed, and from our own observations in various workplaces in the U.S., South America, Asia, and Europe, we developed the categorization below, again based on external, integrated, and internal factors.

Because of the nature of the topic, which is the organization, we refer to the external factors in this case as *environmental factors,* pertaining to the society and industry in which the company operates. We refer to the internal factors as *people-related,* pertaining to the organization's workforce. We further distinguish internal factors with two sub categories: leaders and subordinates.

Some of the environmental elements present in an organization that consciously attempts to nurture spirituality in the workplace are, according to many sources, an appealing aesthetic atmosphere (plants, ornaments, books), order, and inspiring quotations.

Some of the integrated elements we identified in a spiritually attuned organization are peace, comfort, a generally pleasant representation, accessibility to information, a certain level of informality (lack of stern protocol), the existence of pleasant organizational subcultures such as clubs and organizational functions, fair compensation and good reward mechanisms, and the organization's involvement in charity projects in the community.

The internal (people-related) factors present in an organization that nurtures a spiritual mindset follow:

1. From a leadership point of view: top executives who are sensitive, kind, and aware of the humane factor, reflected in their creation of a caring environment and a high level of flexibility in accessing different levels of the organization;

2. From all employees' point of view: the reflection of the leaders' spiritual intent in the workplace; the presence of kind people; high levels of interaction; team performance; involvement (meetings, encouraging mental contributions); conviviality among employees; the appearance of an increased bonding among all workers through commonality in character, which manifests itself in generally accepted high ethical and moral standards as well as the presence of a "giver" culture rather than a "taker" culture; a tradition of helping one another; an attitude of prioritizing collective over personal goals; trust; respect; valuing differences; a focus on solutions instead of problems; the availability of mentors; and a sense of mission that goes beyond the bottom line.

> *Every man is like the company he is wont to keep.*
>
> Euripides

Table 9.1 on the next page presents the above points in a systematic manner.

## Transforming the Workplace into a Spiritual One

Organizations, like people, can change over time. In order to identify some of the most apparent causes of organizational transformation, we asked the participants in our various studies the following question: "What are some of the organizational reasons that could influence the transformation from a workplace that does not consciously attempt to nurture spirituality and the human spirit to one that does?" We furthered our findings with personal observations and literature review.

Table 9.1. When an organization consciously attempts to nurture spirituality in the workplace, what is present?

| Environment (External) | Environment/ People (Integrated) | People (Internal) | |
| --- | --- | --- | --- |
| | | Leadership | All workers |
| • Aesthetic environment <br> • Order <br> • Motivational affirmations | • Peace <br> • Comfort <br> • Pleasant representation <br> • Accessibility of information <br> • Informality (lack of protocol) <br> • Clubs and organizational functions <br> • Fair compensation and good reward mechanisms <br> • Charity from the organization to the community | • Sensitive, kind top executives <br> • Access to different levels of the organization | • Kind people <br> • Interaction <br> • Team performance <br> • Involvement <br> • More bonding of people, through commonality in character <br> • Reflection of the leader's spiritual intent in the workplace <br> • Helping one another <br> • Prioritizing collective over personal goals <br> • Trust <br> • Respect <br> • Valuing differences <br> • Focusing on solutions instead of problems <br> • Mentors <br> • A sense of mission that goes beyond the bottom line <br> • Harmony among employees |

Most of our findings demonstrated that the main reason for an organizational transformation is the occurrence of an experience, either for the organization, its leaders, or one of its employees, that changes the perspectives of the entire group and elicits an approach within the organization that will be more attuned to a spiritual mindset.

Listed below are some of the main transformation instigators we encountered in our studies, observations, and readings:

- **Unfavorable company developments.** The 9/11 terrorist attacks come to mind: When businesses experience such traumatic occurrences, their leaders and employees develop a tendency to reevaluate the organizational values, and, when necessary, redefine them.
- **Life-changing occurrences in the lives of key people in the organization.** This factor may also result in a reconsidered business approach. In this case, the occurrences do not necessarily have to be traumatic. They can also be positive, such as exposure to successful organizations that have already adopted the spiritual practice or organizational cultures from abroad that have proven successful over time.
- **Unfavorable internal developments.** If the company has practiced a rigid hierarchical approach before, but finds that it only results in high turnover and absenteeism, the leaders may consider a more spiritual approach.
- **Favorable outcomes from an attempted interactive approach.** This may also cause company management to rethink its policies and strategies, facilitating a more interactive approach in the future.

In general, the majority of our sources agreed that an organizational transformation could only be triggered by a significant experience and not merely by attending a seminar or reading a brochure. The experience, as mentioned above, could be personal or organizational, positive or negative, industry-based or intra-organizational.

> *An organizational transformation will only be triggered through experience, be it personal or organizational, positive or negative, internal or external.*

Based on the previously presented and discussed categorization, we grouped the answers given by the various interviewees into theme clusters, which were initially only based on internal and external factors. In this particular case, we designated the main external factor *Organizational Circumstances*, and the main internal factor, *Personal Circumstances*. However, during the listing of these structures, we found that both categories could be classified further by using the same distinction principle of external and internal factors. For the organizational circumstances, we listed the external drivers under *Organizational Experiential*, while we listed the internal drivers as *Leadership Experiential*.

We did not list an integrated category for this topic because this particular issue calls for answers that merely pertain to either internal or external aspects—no in-betweens.

The final result of our clustering procedure is presented in Table 9.2. Preceding this table is a narrative presentation of the findings:

The organizational influences behind the transformation of a workplace that does not consciously attempt to nurture spirituality into one that does can be classified into two main causes:

1. Organizational-Experiential, in which it may be that unfavorable company developments (deterioration of morale, productivity, efficiency) call for reconsideration of the organizational rules of existence;
2. Leadership-Experiential, in which the transformation may be instigated by a change in leadership perspectives, an unforeseen tragic event involving the leader, or the leader's desire to attract good people (employees and customers) to the business, and thus enhance the quality of life in the work environment.

Table 9.2. Organizational reasons that could influence the transformation from a non-spiritual to a spiritual workplace.

| Organizational Circumstances | |
|---|---|
| Organizational-Experiential | Leadership-Experiential |
| • Unfavorable company developments (deterioration of morale, productivity, efficiency) that call for reconsideration of the organizational rules of existence<br><br>• Favorable company developments when attempting a more integrative approach | • A change in leadership perspectives<br><br>• An unforeseen tragic event<br><br>• The will to attract good people (workers and customers) to the business<br><br>• The leader's will to change, to enhance the quality of life in the work environment |

## Managerial Actions toward the Establishment of a Spiritual Workplace

It would be appropriate at this point to review some actions an organization's management can take toward enhancing the level of spirituality in their workplace. It is important to note that such a positive transformation does not always happen smoothly. There are factors that make it easy to live in alignment with spiritual values in the workplace, but there are also factors that make it difficult to do so.

The ease of living in alignment with spiritual values in the workplace entails internal and external elements, as well as elements that integrate the internal and external categories.

Some of the internal elements that make living in alignment with spiritual values in the workplace easy include 1) freeing one's self from an egocentric mindset; 2) having the spiritual mindset as a natural part instead of a learned one; 3) being open-minded; 4) living with one's real self without having to maintain multiple personas; and 5) the consequential personal fulfillment that the attainment of these elements bring. These factors can come easily to those who already have a tendency to share, cooperate, and help others toward improvement in life. The factors may, however, be more difficult for those who tend to favor a hyper-individualistic approach in a harsh, controlling, and spiteful work environment where everyone seems to be out to harm everyone else—environments where the underlying assumption is that there can be no winner without a loser.

> *If you knew what I know about the power of giving, you would not let a single meal pass without sharing it in some way.*
>
> Buddha

Some of the integrated elements that would be internally and externally identifiable and could make living in alignment with spiritual values in the workplace easy include 1) acquiring a feeling of trust that enables one to relax; and 2) being caring, loving, and supportive of others. However, here too we have to state that these elements require a receptive environment. Harsh work environments as described above, where everyone is out to undercut everyone else, do not lend themselves to such spiritually oriented behavior.

Some of the external elements that could make living in alignment with spiritual values in the workplace easy involve reciprocal acceptance and appreciation from people who are in tune with each other and therefore get along better, which enables the creation of a more pleasant atmosphere. Here again, the environment must be receptive toward this behavior.

In general we can conclude that the ease of living in alignment with spiritual values in a workplace is derived from encouraging employees to remain their own wholesome self and to act accordingly.

> *The ease of living in alignment with spiritual values in a workplace is derived from encouraging employees to remain their own wholesome self and to act accordingly.*

The difficulty of living in alignment with spiritual values in the workplace can also be traced back to internal and external elements, as well as factors that integrate the internal and external categories.

Some of the internal elements that can make living in alignment with spiritual values in the workplace difficult include 1) erasing the pile of negative consciousness that one has generated over years of living, such as having been exposed to discrimination, denigration, or deceit; 2) going through hard times, which can cause someone to fall prey to various malicious acts such as stealing, cheating, lying, or backstabbing colleagues to get ahead; and 3) being harder on one's self, which can be related to the desire to lead by example and apply a form of the golden rule ("do *not* unto others what you do *not* want others to do unto you").

Some of the integrated elements—those that are internally and externally identifiable—that can make living in alignment with spiritual values in the workplace difficult are 1) obtaining the awareness of karma, which boils down to the application of the golden rule ("do unto others as you want them to do unto you"), particularly if you were never used to think that way; and 2) the process of immersing your real self into a massive organizational structure that has different priorities. The latter may be particularly difficult if you find no compatibility between your values and the organization's priorities. It is highly probable that a spiritual worker with high morals will exit such an organization and search for a more compatible work environment.

Some of the external elements that can make living in alignment with spiritual values in the workplace difficult involve 1) a decline in work efficiency when an employee with good intentions is deceived by malicious customers or colleagues at the organization's expense (in other words, people who dishonor your trust); and 2) in general, the worker's attempts to obtain trust, since most workplaces do not encourage or exhibit qualities that are aligned with the spiritual mindset. A possible result of the latter difficulty is the chance of being ostracized by peers in the organization if you refuse to participate in immoral practices.

As a finale to this part of the chapter, we present a statement made by an executive we interviewed during our studies that we believe could clarify the role of management in attaining and sustaining a spiritual mindset at work. The executive's perspective addresses an issue that has been dormant in the minds of corporate people who oppose the idea of applying spirituality in the workplace.

> *The difficult part of living in alignment with spiritual values at work is, that the easy part— being one's own wholesome self—is unnatural to the business organization.*

Neal explained it as the fear within business executives of the S-word (spirituality), because it is often confused with the R-word (religion).(88) Mitroff and Denton explained it as a "values-based organization," which considers itself aligned with neither religion nor spirituality, and even rejects both concepts in strong terms, yet demonstrates an implicit definition of the spiritual work-mindset in its operations despite its denial.(89) The executive stated:

> The difficult part of living in alignment with spiritual values at work is that the easy part—being one's own wholesome self—is unnatural to the business organization. So in a very pragmatic way you hit the difficult part, because most organizations do not have the education to understand what you're doing when you educate business doers to pursue whatever strategy is appropriate to maximize the profitability and return on investment in that company. They have always been focused on the quantity of life: the bottom line; whatever it takes to get there, and give your stockholders and shareholders their profit— that's what they do. So, we have always trained people to do that, rather than pursue quality of life, which can get you to the same place through a different process. But the difficult part is, that in your attempt to achieve a higher quality of life while still focusing on the bottom line, you run into that culture and that mentality, which basically is suspect of what you're talking about: "How can that work? How can that be? How can you be a reasonably decent person in a business organization?" Because, see what we do now: we separate our lives. If I'm a normal business executive, which I'm not, I'd have my business life, and I'd have my personal life. And many times the two don't meet. In my personal life I am the kind of person I want to be. In my business life I am the kind of person I have to be. Thus, the

difficulty is transferring who you really are into this massive organizational structure that has different priorities. That's the difficult part. And the difficult part is, at the same time, not being ostracized by your peers in the organization. You know: "What are you talking about? Where have you been? What are you smoking?" So that's the difficult part, but that's the challenging part as well.

> *Out-of-the-office events are valuable for the establishment of interconnectedness among workers, because such events enable people to get to know each other outside the work setting, discover each other's additional talents, and learn to value and see each other as complete human beings.*

Our findings as shared above emphasize the importance of management's engagement in making spirituality in the workplace succeed. In order to establish a work environment that meets the requirements of a spiritual one, the people involved, starting with those in leadership positions, should make sure that they perceive each other as more than just elements in a production process. This should be stressed as a company policy. The awareness of colleagues as people is enhanced when there is regular planning and execution of social events outside the workplace, activities that, as discussed in Chapter 2, have decreased over the years for understandable reasons. Re-implementing such activities on a large scale would certainly require a comprehensive reevaluation of our levels of endurance toward one another. However, out-of-the-office events are valuable for the establishment of interconnectedness among employees because such events enable people to get to know each other outside the work setting, discover each other's additional talents, and learn to value and see each other as complete human beings.(90) The organization of events should also be specifically incorporated in the company's policy.

Finally, the creation of aesthetically pleasant surroundings, as far as the workplace allows it, should not be underestimated.(91) We should also emphasize the importance of accessibility to information and leaders, as it generates an enormous amount of trust and motivation within employees. These two points should also be worded in the company's policy.

If there is no problem in approaching supervisors and managers, and if there is no rigid hierarchical setting to be detected, the overall spirit in the workplace is enhanced, and employees develop an increased determination to perform at their very best.(92)

129

## General Recommendations for Organizations

As Mitroff and Denton stated in *A Spiritual Audit of Corporate America*, organizations can develop a mentality that supports the realization of spirituality in the workplace, even if they refuse to be called "spiritual workplaces," yet still operate according to a strong set of values such as awareness, consciousness, dignity, honesty, openness, respect, integrity, and trust.

### Internal behavior
An organization achieves its highest level of performance if a spiritual mindset is established and maintained among its employees. Like one of the executives we interviewed during our studies eloquently stated,

> When you employ spirituality and leave room for discussing it, you can far exceed the normal business profit and return parameters that are occurring under the current way of doing business. By using the process of spirituality and by beginning to enhance creativity and innovativeness and taking people to different levels, the end result can be far better returns than what we have today because we're multiplying productivity so much.

Organizational leaders should be encouraged to create room for cultivating a spiritual mindset among employees by enabling acceptance, respect, understanding, appreciation, trust, involvement, support, mentoring, ethical practices, team settings, and perspective sharing.

Each organization is ultimately led by individuals, so what counts for a person in achieving a spiritual workplace should also count for an organization: regular social events, greater accessibility to information and people in the organization, and an aesthetically pleasant environment to the extent possible given the organization's activities and financial capacities.

Organizational leaders should also ensure that employees experience motivation through a reciprocal flow from the organization. The guarantee of recognition and appropriate rewards for employees' input also enhances job satisfaction and self-esteem within the spiritual worker.

> *Each organization is ultimately led by individuals, so what counts for a person in order to achieve a spiritual workplace should also count for an organization: love and connection.*

## External behavior

In reviewing the external behavior of an organization that engages in spiritual behavior, the following statement from a business executive we interviewed during our research seems appropriate:

> If you broaden the definition of what the workplace should be to include, for example, the community in which the organization functions, you will see that a lot of these same characteristics also hold in terms of relating to other members of the larger community. If you function this way you actually engender trust. The community will benefit from the exposure to that kind of behavior. So spiritually attuned behavior should govern the relationship not only within your organization, but also between your organization and others outside, for every business is the product of a network, including customers, suppliers, employees, etc. So, in a way you cannot just function within your organization alone. It's impossible. Behaving spiritually is a way to become part of this entire network. And people who behave in the spiritual way, and feel strongly about it, draw others toward that behavior.

This statement captures an important organizational recommendation: If the spiritual mindset is expanded and translated in the organization's behavior toward the world outside, the entire community in which the organization operates will benefit. Therefore, an organization should establish an atmosphere of fairness, cooperativeness, vision, responsibility, charity, creativeness, high productivity, and accomplishment (see Figure 7.1).

## The cultural issue

According to a large number of authors on the topic such as Chopra, Wheatley, Mitroff and Denton, and Neal, a spiritual workplace is one where people bring in their whole self, not just a part, and are appreciated for who and what they are—completely, without any distinction of rank or position.

Jingshen is the Mandarin word for spirit and vivacity. It is an important word for those who would lead, because above all things, spirit and vivacity set effective organizations apart from those that will decline and die.

James L. Hayes

Yet, as Mitroff and Denton also point out, our Western way of thinking may very well be the major hurdle toward establishing the holistic approach that a spiritual workplace calls for. In Chapter 2 (see under the heading *"The Paradox of Contemporary Workplace Mentality"*) we referred to this problem within the scope of the organization internally. In this section, we review the issue in a broader perspective, that is, as a social mindset that might have to be reevaluated.

As mentioned in Chapter 2, the lack of spiritual approaches in the workplace can be traced back to the American culture of individualism. In the individualistic perspective, people are encouraged to focus solely on their own advancement, even at the cost of others. This trend is not only displayed at the personal level, but also at the organizational level. Within business corporations, the individualistic perspective requires employees to practice extreme caution with their personal issues, as these could be used against them. Thus the question: Is it even possible to establish a spiritual workplace where people bring their entire *being* in, are valued for all of their input and all they represent, and feel content with the *meaning* they find in this environment?

> *Our Western way of thinking may very well be the major hurdle to establishing the holistic approach that a spiritual workplace calls for.*
>
> Ian Mitroff
> and Elizabeth Denton

Workplace politics is the most obvious bottleneck that comes to mind here. Our culture has trained us to be competitive and ambitious. Very few of us would ever discard an opportunity to get a promotion, even if we knew that one of our colleagues deserves it more. Strategies to make progress in today's aggressive work environment sometimes involve elbowing the kinder-hearted ones around us out of the way, and becoming close buddies with the ones we perceive as potential gateways to the top, even if we do not really like them. How much more insincere could it get? Nevertheless, our culture has taught us that this is justified. Only the strong survive. So how, then, could this mindset align with a spiritual one?

It is, after all, this very phenomenon called workplace politics that makes it unattractive for the well-intentioned ones among us to bring our entire self into work, since that would mean providing openness about ourselves, exposing our most vulnerable sides, and, hence, allowing the sharks that oftentimes swim in the corporate ocean to take a huge bite out of our souls.

Therefore, if a spiritual workplace is one where we should be able to be our entire selves, we should consider whether we will have to change our cultural mindset first. At the risk of sounding gloomy, that will not be an overnight process. In the meantime, we should realize that it is a beautiful thing to bring our entire soul into work, but we should do so with a certain level of caution, because at this point we still have to be aware of the fact that everyone has a different personal agenda, perhaps even one that consistently opposes ours.

So we end this section with a daring note: Maybe our age-old capitalistic mindset, which gave us a certain understanding of "rational goals," needs some socialistically oriented adjustment, since it may ultimately turn out to be the greatest deterrence to a spiritual workplace. Perhaps we are in need of a new perspective here—not capitalism, socialism, communism, or Marxism, but a new perception of "commonism," which we could define as *the establishment of a common perspective about the values for each and every one of us in life.*

> People are the only assets in an organization that will multiply their output to dazzling levels if their managers can demonstrate that they genuinely value not only the workers' contributions, but their very being in the work environment.

## Motivation

It cannot be stressed enough: People are the only assets in an organization that will multiply their output to dazzling levels if their managers can demonstrate that they genuinely value not only the employees' contributions, but their very being in the work environment. In order to guide an organization through the most difficult times, every leader should therefore be aware of these important realities about motivation and rewards:

1. Motivation is what you do to improve your employees' performance. Make it a habit to regularly walk around on the production floor. Talk to them. Show interest. Ivory towers are cold, lonely, and hopelessly outdated.
2. The best motivation you can give is to inform your employees about the firm's competitive environment. Share the bigger picture! Do not think they lack the intelligence to comprehend what is happening. If you explain things clearly enough, and encourage them to ask questions while you do so, they will feel more attached.
3. Provide extrinsic rewards (the ones *you* give them—a raise, some praise, training, awards) that stimulate their intrinsic rewards (the ones *they* feel—their job satisfaction, personal development, or self-control). If you do not know all the details, talk to somebody who does in order to make the right decisions regarding the most effective rewards.
4. Realize that people are different from one another. There is no single way of rewarding everybody; what motivates one can be a turn-off for another. Again, talk to their immediate supervisor or

others who work closely with them if you do not have the time to figure it out yourself.

5. Try to detect where people excel and do as much as you can to make them productive in that particular area. If you want people to do a good job, give them a good job to do. Does that not say it all?

6. Make sure that you set achievable yet challenging goals and that you have sufficient and attainable rewards for the employees who reach them. A job that is too easy becomes dull and may cause the employee to become distracted. A job that is too hard is discouraging and may cause the employee to become insecure. Both outcomes can impede the company's advancement. So, even if it takes some time to find out what the best job is for an employee, invest in the effort, for it will be an investment worth your while—and the company's as well.

> *Make sure that you set achievable yet challenging goals and that you have sufficient and attainable rewards for the employees who reach them.*

7. If you know how to disapprove of bad performance, make sure you also know how to show approval of good and improving performance. The biggest turn-off for an employee who tries to improve is to feel that his or her attempts go unrecognized. So never forget the word of encouragement, no matter how small the progress.

8. Remember that money is but one of the many ways to reward people. And it is not even the most important or effective one. Accommodating ways for employees to reach their goals is often valued higher.

9. Attune your rewards to your employees' physical, emotional, and intellectual needs. This boils down again to what was stated in the first item of this list: talk to them!

10. Leave room for people to have a voice in the firm's strategies toward reaching goals. They often know better than you what the customers want. Listening cannot hurt. And remember: recognition is still the best reward.

## Creating constructive stress

The word stress has become synonymous with every negative emotion we feel, especially when pertaining to the workplace. However, this is only partially correct, because stress can have positive effects as well. In fact, it does so all the time! The problem is just that we do not recognize our driving motives toward high performance as stress-related.

In order to link stress to spirituality in the workplace, we will first have to provide some clarification about the two phenomena.

It is not hard to comprehend that stress has two faces, a constructive and a destructive one. Schermerhorn describes the constructive version of stress as the one we need in order to obtain performance excellence: It enhances the quality of our work and encourages us to work harder and become better at what we do. Destructive stress, on the other hand, is the infamous one that we dread because it puts excessive pressure on us, which can lead to low performance, absentee-ism, burn out, low self-esteem, or even withdrawal.(93)

> If people are provided with work that brings about the right amount of stress within them, meaning that it represents an interesting challenge to their capabilities, they will undoubtedly like what they do. Job satisfaction will be established in their lives and their mood at work as well as outside will improve.

That explained, the conclusion could be drawn that every spiritually oriented manager should try to detect how much stress each one of his or her employees can handle. Understandably, this will vary from one to another. However, it is worth the time and effort for the following reason: If people are provided with work that brings about the right amount of stress within them, meaning that it represents an interesting challenge to their capabilities and creates an opportunity to prove themselves, as well as the motivation to obtain training in order to perform even better, they will undoubtedly like what they do. This circumstance results not only in enhanced job satisfaction, but also a general feeling of well-being in- and outside the workplace. Besides, they will increasingly feel better about themselves knowing that they are valued for what they do and that their efforts and progress are recognized.

With this enumeration of experiences we practically confirm the existing concept of a spiritual workplace, one where everybody is happy, motivated, and respected. A simpler cycle is hard to come up with: constructive stress leads to constructive behavior and, con-sequently, a constructive workplace. That is how stress can add to the spirituality in your workplace.

### Strategy review
The theme of strategies is an interesting one, especially when perceived against the background of facilitating a spiritual workplace. What is a strategy, really? It is the way you choose to get from your current point to the one you desire. If you look at it that way, you

actually develop strategies all the time, even if you call it something else.

When it comes to company strategies, we should emphasize some points with regard to spirituality in the workplace:

1.  All companies have to develop a strategy. However, due to the fact that everything changes so rapidly these days, strategies need to be flexible and adjustable; goals will have to be modified as well. After all, if the target changes, so does the road that leads to it.
2.  Many company executives still make the mistake of hanging on to a strategy that has been dead for quite some time. They are willing to blame everything for the mishaps the organization is going through, as long as it is not their strategy. Spiritual companies are aware of this perceptional trap and make sure they do not fall into it.

    > *Strategies are not one-size-fits-all. Developing a strategy requires insight in where the organization currently stands; where it wants to go; and how it wants to get there.*

3.  Strategies are not one-size-fits-all. Developing a strategy requires insight into where the organization currently stands; where it wants to go; and how it wants to get there. The industry in which the organization operates also has its influence on the strategy. Does the organization focus on growth, on maintenance of its current position, or on reduction of activities? In other words, what stage are the organization and its products in?
4.  As Hamel said, strategies are nice, but clinging to a strategy as if it is one's life is wrong. Much of a company's success will depend on vision, luck, and the establishment of a spiritual approach, even more so than strategy!
5.  In order to develop the right strategy, one has to look at the company's internal and external conditions; in other words, one will need to make a SWOT analysis, which consists of a listing of strengths and weaknesses (the internal parts), and opportunities and threats (the external parts). Only when the company's leaders have the full picture of where the organization stands and what goes on in the industry can they decide how to make their move— and in which direction.

The way a business organization handles its strategies and policies is a great contributor to the level of its success. The leaders of a spiritual workplace are aware of that, and ensure that optimal involvement and accessibility are applied at all levels of the organization, together with the next point of review—communication.

## Communication in management

Communication may very well be considered the success factor or breakpoint in work relationships. Good managers and organizational leaders know that communication should be effective (well understood) and efficient (performed in the fastest, most economical, and most concise way).

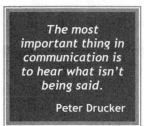

*The most important thing in communication is to hear what isn't being said.*

Peter Drucker

Various factors can disturb the communication process. We classify those disturbing factors as *noise*. Noise can be anything, from misunderstanding the use of language to the use of an inappropriate medium for the communication.

Spiritually attuned managers have to know what types of messages they should send through email, phone, reports, or face-to-face meetings: a complicated or sensitive message would preferably be conveyed in a face-to-face setting with room for response or requests for clarification; a routine message, on the other hand, could be handled through email or phone conversation.

The medium a manager chooses to communicate will depend on various factors such as time limitations, budgets, locations, or the intellectual level of the receivers.

The manager's personality can also support or hinder communication. A manager should therefore know his or her strengths, and use them—as well as his or her weaknesses, and improve on them.

In a spiritual workplace, the most important elements of good communication are: clarity, honesty, brevity, listening, and feedback.

- Clarity: Make sure the other party understands the message. Sometimes people are afraid or embarrassed to admit that they did not understand your statements. Spiritual workers should be encouraged to ask if they are unclear about a task or assignment.

- Honesty: Be straightforward and open. If employees catch their manager telling a lie, even if it was with the best intentions, they may start mistrusting him or her, which hinders future communication.

- Brevity: Communication that is too wordy can confuse the receivers. A spiritual manager states his or her point, restates it, then asks if he or she was understood. This manager avoids engaging in endless preaching at all times.

- Listening: Spiritual leaders are alert to what the receiver says—or does not say! They pay close attention to the body language of the other party while conveying their message. Also, the spiritual leader knows that giving other parties time and room to bring up their points is invaluable in establishing high-quality and lasting work relationships.

- Feedback: Open and timely communication allows for a regular stream of feedback in order to continuously improve operations.

As time progresses, so do the communication methods. Managers should beware, though, of using high-tech communication tools with a workforce that is not ready for them. Spiritual managers, finally, also remember that it is preferable to spend some extra time and money on getting the message across sufficiently than to have entire—and sometimes expensive or urgent—work pro- cesses repeated due to a small misunder- standing.

> *To keep your lips from slips, five things observe with care: to whom you speak, of whom you speak, and how, and when, and where.*
>
> Unknown

## Leadership

In a recent survey among leadership students, we generated an interesting compilation of considerations for leaders who want to enhance the quality of life in their workplace. These leaders should consider:

- Mission and vision: The strength of a leader starts with having a clearly defined purpose in life.

- Conviction: This includes the most appropriate leadership style, given the conviction.

- Communication skills: These should align followers more closely with the organization's goals.

- Awareness: This means paying attention current circumstances, the people who follow the vision, the leader-follower respect level, and the desired result.

- Humility: Arrogant leaders are not be followed for long because they intimidate their followers, which interferes with the quality of mutual communication and sharing the conviction. Once followers turn away, the leader ceases to be a leader. On the other hand, a leader who is humble enough to give followers credit for their efforts is honored and respected in return.

- Adaptability: Nothing hastens a downfall faster than a stubborn, inflexible leader who is unable to respond to changing environments.

- People skills: This means knowing how to deal with followers from various backgrounds, and thus, with various perceptions.

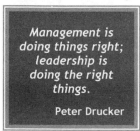

*Management is doing things right; leadership is doing the right things.*

Peter Drucker

- Well-rounded personality: The ability to get along with people and show sympathy, knowledge, and stability.

- Understanding: Although this factor ties into adaptability and people skills, it still deserves special attention, as understanding pertains to much more than just working well with followers—it encompasses the entire environment in which the leader leads.

- Motivating skills: It is not always easy to bring a group of people up to the same interest level. Different followers may have different perceptions and different capacities, and therefore may need different tactics to get things done.

- Ethics: Before leading anyone, the leader should make sure his or her intentions and values are in the right place.

- Inspiration: This is closely related to conviction, communication, and motivation. The leader should believe in him- or herself, be able to get the message across, and live it in order to get the followers to do the same.

- Honesty: If a leader is caught lying once, his or her integrity is lost, as is the trust of the followers.

- Kindness: The leader should be accessible and friendly, because these manifestations encourage followers to open up and share their suggestions and experiences, which could turn out to be valuable resources to the leader.

- Charisma: Although maybe not the most important asset for a leader to consider, charisma helps to get people moving toward the goal at a steadier pace.

- Determination: Once the goal is set, the leader should be confident and resolute in achieving it, in spite of some hurdles that will undoubtedly surface.

- Sensitivity: It takes a strong leader to show empathy for others' needs and give support and understanding without becoming overwhelmed by others' problems.

- Responsible risk-taking: This takes courage as well, but is crucial. A good leader should follow his or her beliefs, even when the odds are against him or her. At the same time, the leader should stay on the right side of the fine line between taking calculated risks and indulging in foolish recklessness.

> If you lead the people with correctness, who will dare not be correct?
>
> Confucius

- Decisiveness: The ability to make bold decisions when necessary can determine the difference between mediocrity and greatness.

- Heart: It is the heart that drives every part of an individual. A good heart shows strength of character—not weakness.

- Support: A leader offers his or her followers guidance in every possible form. Mentoring may be one of them. Facilitating training to enhance followers' skills is another.

- Goals: If the goals of the organization are not congruent with the values of the leader, the leader should either change these goals or exit the organization.

- Hard work and dedication: Although this is often thought of more as a management skill than a leadership trait, it still works miracles in bonding followers to their leader.

- Respect: If followers feel appreciated and respected for their input, they are encouraged to perform even better.

- Listening: Followers often have very useful information to share. They also appreciate a leader who lends an ear to their personal concerns.

- Caring: A leader who listens should also follow up by attempting to improve the quality of his or her followers' lives.

- Optimism: When a positive attitude rubs off on followers, they make the seemingly impossible possible.

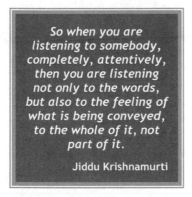

> *So when you are listening to somebody, completely, attentively, then you are listening not only to the words, but also to the feeling of what is being conveyed, to the whole of it, not part of it.*
>
> Jiddu Krishnamurti

- Encouraging followers even when they fail: A good leader does not shy away from giving a reprimand, but does not dwell on it either. He or she tries to catch people doing good things, and mentions that to them as well.

- Social responsibility: The golden rule should be invoked here also as an important leadership consideration: "Do unto others as you would want them to do unto you." This includes being cognizant of the example leaders set with their behavior toward employees as well as customers and peers.

- Knowledge: Knowing the followers and the situation is prerequisite to applying the right leadership strategies.

- Calm: Being calm and collected radiates trust to all stakeholders.

- Patience: This is the trait that ultimately delivers the rewards.

It is needless to say that our list of leadership strategies to improve quality of life in the workplace could continue inexhaustibly. However, the above points may encourage you to add your own perspectives.

### In Review

An excellent way to summarize the points made in this chapter is to present some of the findings of one of our studies conducted among business executives, educational administrators, and entrepreneurs. These individuals provided the following interesting and widely divergent set of answers to the question: "How can spirituality in the workplace be achieved?"

- By admitting that the prevailing focus in our current culture, capitalism and free enterprise, which encourages competition, should be enriched with more humanity;

- Through insight and time spent with all concerned;
- Through national and business school recognition that this new system (spirit @ work) works; but at the same time through the realization that trends take a long time to be realized;
- Through change from within as well as without or above;
- Through committing to and learning to "let go" of controlling things in order to maintain status;
- Through the encouragement of delegating, team performance, and collaboration;
- Through employing reflective, creative, group-focused conversation and consensus building, decision making and processing tools and structures within the workplace in business and education (i.e., the old military-industrial education system is highly resistant to change);
- Through leadership that sets an example of trust, honesty, and kindness, and expects the same from one's colleagues and employees;
- By ensuring that the traits of firmness without cruelty, as well as responsibility, are respected;
- By ensuring that rewards are generous in praise, advancement in position, and financial remuneration, yet earned;
- Through increasing and encouraging teamwork, while consistently remaining respectful of and open to the individual's point of view, and his or her rights to challenge any premise, no matter how different or unique their point of view may be;
- By creating a "marriage" of employers and their employees by developing a means for employers and employees to devise and share common goals and means to achieve them;
- Through the provision of honest opportunities, realistic challenges (including "impossible" ones that are acknowledged as such), support for efforts, and meaningful criticism;
- Through leaders' awareness of the employees' work experience; through their willingness to examine the assumptions behind current practices; and their receptiveness toward developing and embracing new thinking where they find a need. It is the intention that leaders will then lead (and model) the changes necessary to unleash the power of each individual to contribute, while enhancing the employee's loyalty and commitment to the work of the organization. At the same time the leaders will be assisting individuals to achieve their own personal fulfillment.

> *Nature without culture can often do more to deserve praise than culture without nature.*
>
> Cicero

> *Spirit @ work is
> established through
> leadership that sets an
> example of trust,
> honesty and kindness,
> and expects the same
> from one's colleagues
> and employees.*

---

### Reflection Sheet

These areas represent the contents of this chapter that I consider applicable to my life:

_____
_____
_____
_____
_____
_____
_____
_____

These areas represent the contents of this chapter whose applicability to my life I question:

_____
_____
_____
_____
_____
_____
_____
_____
_____
_____

My personal opinions after reading this chapter:

_____
_____
_____
_____
_____
_____
_____

What I would like to remember:

_____
_____
_____
_____
_____
_____
_____
_____

## Chapter 10

# Employee and Other Stakeholder Involvement

> Spirituality in the workplace may have to be initiated by management and policymakers, but the human resource department should definitely be closely involved in the activities that will lead to the sustenance of this trend through the involvement of all stakeholders.
>
> In this chapter we will review some viewpoints that we gathered about HR's involvement in the establishment of a spiritual mindset in the work environment. We will review some practical suggestions and incorporate findings from various studies on the sustenance of spirituality in the workplace.

## The Changing Position of HR

K inicki and Williams maintain that human resource management consists of the activities managers perform to plan for, attract, develop, and retain an effective workforce.(94) However, the work environment, and therefore the appropriate strategies for successful HR management, are rapidly changing. Ross McDonald, a senior lecturer in the Management and Employment Relations department at the University of Auckland, identifies two main factors as significant in this change:

*Adequate and conscientious HR management establishes and retains a qualified, well-cooperating workforce, and therefore, an increase in organizational growth, efficiency, and profitability.*

1. The declining influence of traditional religions (particularly in the West), with their wealth of signs and symbols which provide a constant reminder of agreed-upon laws and ways of acting;

2. A public concern over issues such as modern competitive business practices and globalization [which results in] a cheapening of deeper spiritual values, and their conversion into fleeting management tools or fads.(95)

## HR Management in a Successful Organization

HR management is an often underestimated task in work-environments. However, it is adequate and conscientious HR management that establishes and retains a qualified, well-cooperating workforce, and therefore, an increase in organizational growth, efficiency, and profitability.

The most important tasks of the Human Resource department are to make sure that the people working in and interacting with the organization 1) feel satisfied; 2) are in the right job; and 3) get the opportunity to upgrade their skills when necessary.

Of course it is also HR's task to coordinate the recruitment of new employees for vacant positions. This brings up the interesting point of internal recruiting versus external recruiting. Both have their advantages and disadvantages. Yet, it is the HR department, together with the particular department management, that determines which way to go in certain cases. Here is the dilemma in a nutshell:

- Hiring people internally can be advantageous in that that they are already familiar with the culture and the work climate. It provides employees the positive reinforcement that there are possibilities for promotion in the company; also, it is time- and cost-efficient due to the internal process. At the same time, it represents a few disadvantages such as having to retrain the ones that are now performing in the position they were promoted to, and having to fill the positions that fell open through the promotion.

- Hiring externally brings the advantage of drawing in fresh ideas, and saving time and costs by hiring the person with the right skills (no training needed), but it may bring the disadvantage of having to guide this newly hired person through the organization, which can be a time-consuming process. There is also the possibility of discovering that this new person does not fit well in the organization's culture.

> *When the HR department knows what the long-term plans of top management are, it can tailor its hiring requirements toward those plans and save a lot of the hassle that retraining and laying off of employees bring about.*

As has become apparent, there are at least two sides to everything, and it is HR's call, together with departmental management, to figure out the best course of action for any given situation.

Another valuable point to consider in a spiritual workplace is that the HR department should be more involved in strategic decisions of the organization. The reason is, when the HR department knows what the long-term plans of top management are, it can tailor its hiring requirements toward those plans and save a lot of the hassle that retraining and laying off of employees bring about.

And then there is the motivation aspect of retaining the best employees and keeping them satisfied. There are various ways in which managers, with support of the HR department, can generate improved performance from employees.

An interesting way of retaining good employees is the flexibility strategy, in which various work routines are implemented. Today's workplaces are developing all kinds of methods to retain productive employees. These vary from job-sharing (two people filling a 40-hour workweek); to flextime (different people starting and ending their workday at different times, with two primary time slots in which everyone is present); to telecommuting (working from outside the workplace); and more.

> *Different people perform better under different circumstances. Consequently, they get motivated in different ways—what works for one may not work for another.*

The basic message here is that different people perform better under different circumstances, and they also get motivated in different ways—what works for one may not work for another. Managers, in conjunction with HR, should therefore tailor the way they reward employees to these employees' particular preferences; otherwise, a reward can have a reverse effect on an employee's performance.

In light of the motivation issue, several theories come to mind, two of which we will discuss here:

- ✓ Abraham Maslow's hierarchy of needs: This teaches us that, depending on the need-level of an employee, certain rewards will or will not work for him or her. An employee who is at the basic level will probably care more for an extra dollar per hour than an expensive company award, while an employee who is already settled in regard to basic needs, security, safety, and social contacts, may care more for a prestigious title or a wonderful award complete with ceremony.

- ✓ Frederick Herzberg's motivation-hygiene theory: This teaches us that there are different issues at stake when we talk about job satisfaction than when we talk about job dissatisfaction. We will examine Herzberg's theory from a specific HR perspective later in this chapter.

The simple message embedded in all of the above is that people need to be kept satisfied in order to perform well in a workplace. Managers should try to treat all employees fairly and never make the mistake of playing employees against each other, while, at the same time, they should also be aware that the ways in which employees get motivated vary widely. A good rapport between departmental management and HR is therefore recommended, although, unfortunately, not too often implemented often enough.

## The specific role of HR in applying spirituality in the workplace

The October 2003 issue of *HR Focus* claimed that "keeping employees happy is difficult in these times of layoffs, greater workloads, longer hours, and smaller raises, but it isn't impossible." This source clarified that the secret to achieving employees' happiness is "finding out what matters most to your organization's employees, and then providing it. If it makes your employees happy, you'll have a better chance of keeping them, and keeping them more productive and efficient as well." The article suggested the following attention points for management to focus on in order to maintain a satisfied workforce:

- Avoiding layoffs;
- Offering desirable benefits;
- Practicing good communication;
- Giving employees the flexibility to balance work/life issues.[96]

Patrick Kulesa revealed two other issues for HR departments and managers to keep in mind: 1) Top performers pay special attention to high-level issues of corporate leadership; and 2) high performers seek an environment in which their efforts will be rewarded, not with higher pay necessarily, but with enhanced development and career-path opportunities. Kulesa clarified that it is imperative to provide employees with adequate opportunities for career development and growth. He also emphasized that it is of equal importance that senior leaders provide a clear sense of direction, communicate decisions to employees, and are respected by employees. According to Kulesa, high performers' concerns are much more strategic than those of other staff, reaching to the very heart of the organization's purpose, strategy, and positioning in the marketplace.[97]

*It is imperative for an organization to provide its workers with adequate opportunities for career development and growth.*

On the question, "How should employees and managers grapple with the day-to-day issues?" Sharon Weston offered the following suggestion: "One obvious, but sometimes overlooked, approach is for individuals and organizations to pay close attention to each other's core values, especially when recruiting."[98] Shari Caudron underscored this practice by emphasizing, "The path to enlightened HR starts with hiring."(99) In that regard, Richard Hughes, Robert Ginnett and Gordon Curphy suggested that recruiters focus on hiring individuals with high levels of "achievement orientation," which is nothing more than one's tendency to exert effort toward task accomplishment depending on the strength of his or her motive to achieve success.(100)

"There is a heightening expectation that HR will shift its role from simply providing the delivery mechanism to become a new business driver of change," claimed Lawrence Lyons, of Henley Management College. According to Lyons, "HR is the only function with the relevant people focus to create the soft strategies businesses now need to deliver profits. However, unless HR gets its house in order, there is a real danger that other business functions will win the race for the strategic high ground."(101) Like many others, Lyons emphasized the need for companies to align their mission and core values to the kind of people they wish to attract.

> There is a heightening expectation that HR will shift its role from simply providing the delivery mechanism to become a new business driver of change.
>
> Lawrence Lyons

Yet, hiring the right people is just one part of HR's important task. Once the workforce is in place, it is imperative to keep job satisfaction up. In that regard, Neal Chalofsky asserted that "Herzberg's famous motivation-hygiene theory is still relevant." Chalofsky further claimed that the truly great places to work, such as *Fortune's* 100 Best Places to Work, are not great because of their perks and benefits, but because of their organizational cultures and policies that promote meaningful work and a nurturing, supportive workplace.(102)

To clarify, Herzberg explained that job satisfaction and job dissatisfaction are caused by completely different sets of factors. Herzberg basically claimed that, even when job-dissatisfaction is eliminated, job satisfaction may not yet be achieved. His theory states that there are different powers at work in the elimination of job dissatisfaction versus the achievement of job satisfaction. Herzberg found that job dissatisfaction is caused by factors such as poor supervision, bad working conditions, unpleasant colleagues, low salaries, objectionable work policies or procedures, and low job security. Herzberg contended that HR managers should make sure that these matters, which he calls the hygiene factors, are appropriately taken care of. "However, it makes no sense to overdo them, because even if you enhance one of the above-mentioned hygiene factors to a spectacular height, it will not lead to a higher level of job satisfaction."(103)

In regard to enhancing job satisfaction, Herzberg identified achievement, recognition, responsibility, growth, and the nature of the work as significant motivating factors.(104) Herzberg suggested that HR managers first sufficiently satisfy the hygiene factors—without overdoing it—and then seriously emphasize the motivating factors. If this is applied in the right way, which is not always as straightforward and easy as the theory seems to indicate, then performance should improve.(105)

In a discussion of the Colorado-based company Sounds True, Inc., Caudron presented another set of important factors that HR managers should maintain in the organization:

1. Honest and open communication;
2. Extensive use of peer-review processes that allow team members to provide direct feedback to co-workers about how they may be affecting others;
3. The promotion of collaborative decision making so that managers jointly make key business decisions, and departmental teams determine their own best way of working together.

Caudron subsequently emphasized the crucial part of HR's position in establishing a workplace that is pleasant, yet profitable. Maintaining the balance between financial and human goals is not easy. Shift too far in one direction and business suffers; shift too far in the other and morale withers. Caudron therefore affirmed that it is imperative for HR to stay aware of the importance of both goals, and to integrate this awareness into daily business practices. This is what Caudron called "enlightened HR."(106)

> *Enlightened HR: maintaining the balance between financial and human goals.*

However, financial and human goals are not the only factors HR should try to keep in balance. When it comes to the workforce, HR has another important balance issue to maintain. Tredget translated this responsibility as follows: "There are far too many damaged people in workplaces up and down this country. They have suffered through overwork, failing to balance work and home, failing to develop their emotional intelligence and being the victims of a 24-hour work-oriented culture." Suggesting the implementation of spirituality in the workplace in order to reestablish this necessary balance for employees, Tredget explained, "A spiritually friendly workplace will have greater staff-retention rates, so lowering recruitment costs. It will see an increase in creativity and innovation, improved morale, better cooperation and teamwork and superior interface between the organization and its customers."(107)

Chappel offered creative and easy-to-initiate ideas for HR managers to make any company a more spiritually satisfying place at little or no cost. Some of his ideas on how HR can help establish a spiritually satisfying workplace follow:

- Helping employees connect with nature by bringing in natural features (plants, for example);
- Holding outdoor meetings when possible;
- Allowing staff to take exercise breaks to promote physical and spiritual wellness;
- Staging frequent company celebrations to acknowledge milestones and achievements;
- Honoring creative expression by decorating the workplace with employee-made art;
- Creating an evolving mission statement that employees are proud to live by;
- Rotating those allowed to attend outside events;
- Holding meetings in the round, thereby creating feelings of egalitarianism;
- Encouraging employees to get to know each other better (hobbies, likes and dislikes);
- Encouraging employees to take a turn at answering customer correspondence.(108)

DeCenzo and Robbins emphasized that in every organization success is contingent on how well its employees perform. They found that an individual's performance is a function of his or her ability and willingness to do the job. These authors explained that "motivation can be defined as an individual's willingness to exert effort to achieve the organization's goals, conditioned by this effort's ability to satisfy individual needs."(109) David Dorsey agreed with this theory, asserting that "people and companies do well, financially and otherwise, to the degree that their interests match their values." Dorsey claimed, "people need to believe in what they do for a living before they can tap their deepest creative potential."(110) DeCenzo and Robbins advised that, "in order for motivation to occur, Human Resource Management must: analyze jobs properly, and update them regularly; identify what the job incumbent must possess to be successful; and ensure that it has selected the appropriate person for the job."(111) Thad Green suggested that "managers can motivate employees by setting in motion the three conditions required for motivation—confidence, trust, and satisfaction—and by creating an environment that reinforces those conditions."(112)

> *In every organization success is contingent on how well its employees perform.*

DeCenzo and Robbins list, among the various human resource strategies that they suggest, the following:

- Addressing individual differences by focusing on specific needs and accommodating those needs;
- Properly placing employees;
- Setting achievable goals, including continuous feedback;
- Individualizing rewards by realizing that different people appreciate different rewards;
- Rewarding performance of employees when they achieved set goals;
- Using an equitable system by matching rewards to performance;
- Not forgetting money as a way to increase motivation and recognition;
- Enriching jobs by increasing employees' responsibility for planning and self-evaluation of their work;
- Job rotation to make work more diversified;
- Enabling an employee stock ownership program to make employees feel more connected to the organization.(113)

> *The spiritual perspective is already causing a shift in workplace values. This shift is the move from fear [that comes from not being able to speak up and the fear of what other people might think] to cooperation in the workplace.*
>
> Jennifer Laabs

Marci McDonald offered another suggestion for increasing job motivation by offering training programs designed to open spiritual dialogues to unfetter employees' creativity.(114) Cash, Gray, and Rood added "personal leave days" to the list of options, arguing, "while a personal leave day would cost a firm more money, the value to employee morale and company goodwill [among other advantages] could well offset the cost."(115) Caudron suggested "an open company culture through open communication [between employees and the management team]" as a way of increasing motivation.(116) Laabs recommended the formation of "workgroups focusing on coping with the work environment by having a larger perspective on life, [thereby] aiming to find a voice in the workplace." Laabs asserted that "the spiritual perspective is already causing a shift in workplace values. This shift is the move from fear [that comes from not being able to speak up and the fear of what other people might think] to cooperation in the workplace."(117) Laabs stated further that others in the spirituality movement agree that removing fear can help companies achieve peak performance. "As you implement these new values—leaving behind competition, promoting cooperation, making people equal and allowing them to live in a fear-free environment—you'll engage not only people's intuition and creativity; you'll also engage their ownership of the organization."(118)

Rosner cited consultant Martin Rutte, who offered a simple four steps action plan for HR directors to better address spirituality at work:

1. Make it safe, permissible, and comfortable to have the conversation about spirituality in the workplace, if people choose. Begin talking, writing, and communicating in a gentle, non-threatening, non-dogmatic manner. Respect others' points of view and the degree to which they wish to participate.

2. Seek help from the many resources available. There are myriad sources filled with ideas, conferences, books, speakers, [and] discussion groups.

3. Allow a form to evolve to help expand spirituality in your workplace. This can be anything from a regular discussion group to a shared project or activity to a speaker series. Agree on a method and time.

4. Evaluate what is working and what is not working. Then correct what is not working and nurture what is. Do not forget to celebrate.(119)

As the above examples indicate, the application of spirituality in the workplace is very much in line with the newly emerging perspectives on good HR management practices. Following the suggestions from the various sources cited above, *right people, right job, right balance, and right work climate*, should provide a good roadmap to successful HR management, and subsequently, excellence in organizational performance.

As Tredget stated, "Understanding the spiritual will become an important part of workplace human development. It will become part of management training and have great benefits including creating more social stability and increased profitability and productivity."(120)

> *Understanding the spiritual will become an important part of workplace human development.*
>
> Dermot Tredget

Cary Cooper, pro-vice chancellor of the University of Manchester Institute of Science and Technology and a member of the *Human Resource Management International Digest* advisory board, warned "Employees will simply follow the green light to a company with better working practices, and take with them the skills, knowledge, and prospects of the organization they left. The mantra foremost in employers' minds must be, "Lose your staff, and you lose your business."(121)

## HR as the Sustainer of a Spiritual Workplace

Interestingly, we found in our studies that, while management was mainly considered responsible for establishing a spiritual workplace; it was primarily HR responsibilities, executed in conjunction with management, that were mentioned by most of our study participants as the sustaining factors toward such a work environment.

> *Employees will simply follow the green light to a company with better working practices, and take with them the skills, knowledge and prospects of the organization they left.*
>
> Cary Cooper

Below we list respondents' answers to the question, "How can spirituality in the workplace be sustained?"

- Through widespread education to awaken people (consciously), and with tools to keep us awake;
- By first establishing a connection between leadership and staff, and then maintaining this connection through meetings and mentoring, and subsequently offering incentives for making good progress in the trend;
- By participating in a critical mass of successful organizations and models that become visible, compelling, and generative;
- By networking like and diverse groups to demonstrate ability to align values, purpose, and actions; and model acceptance and accommodation of differences;
- By enabling key funding and economic links to provide support and time for the paradigm shifts and documentation of impact—time to realize what is being learned and to practice doing things differently;
- By ensuring individual and team growth through giving recognition, support, and praise in a generous way, so that the entire workplace will advance;
- By regularly adding benefits (not necessarily monetary) to employees' packages on top of those they bought into when they first accepted employment, while, at the same time, challenging employees to devise innovative services and benefits they can offer their employer or company;
- By understanding and maintaining the approach of being at least as productive as those systems that are based primarily on the dollar bottom line, as businesses will, then becoming increasingly

amenable toward adding quality-of-life dimensions to their goals and purposes.

## The Other Stakeholders

Every entity has a set of stakeholders involved in its existence. Human beings do, and organizations do. Stakeholders are, briefly, all those entities (individuals, organizations, communities), that have a stake in the entity's performance. For an organization, stakeholders could include employees and management, as extensively reviewed above, but also suppliers, customers, government organizations involved with the organization's performance, the communities in which the organization operates, competitors, and others.

An organization that values a spiritual mindset attempts to avoid violence in the interaction with all of its stakeholders and strives to improve relationships on all levels. This means that the organization's performance at all levels should be scrutinized. Conscious questions that spiritually oriented organizations should ask themselves in respect to all of their actions include:

> *An organization that values a spiritual mindset attempts to avoid violence in the interaction with all of its stakeholders and strives to improve relationships on all levels.*

✓ Are we listening to our customers, and are we providing them sufficient ways to communicate with us?

✓ Are we trying our best to meet the needs of our customers?

✓ Are we fair in our approach toward suppliers? Are we giving all types of suppliers a chance, and are we not allowing prejudgments to affect our choices?

✓ Are we considering the potential harm certain elements in our production may cause the environments from which they come and/or the environments in which they will be used?

✓ Are we playing fair toward our competitors?

✓ Are we gearing our policies and procedures toward rules and regulations applicable in the areas where we operate?

✓ Are we gearing our policies and procedures toward our own moral values?

&#10003; Are we adequately considering potential harm that our processes could cause toward the environment?

&#10003; Are we giving back enough to the communities in which we operate?

&#10003; Are we contributing toward the overall quality of life on the planet?

These conscious questions represent but a few that spiritually oriented organizations should consider to ensure that the well-being of stakeholders is incorporated into their decisions and actions.

## In Review

Spiritually oriented organizations, as this chapter—and the entire book—demonstrates, have an important set of questions to ask themselves and actions to undertake in order to create and nurture their spiritual existence. However, one needs to understand that once the trend is set, the sustenance should not be too hard to provide. Practice makes perfect. If business organizations, whether for profit or not, succeed in establishing an atmosphere of trust, acceptance, and cooperation into their workplace, employees will adopt this attitude, because it will become part of the organization's culture. Those who do not feel compatible with the spiritual mindset will ultimately exit.

> *Spiritually oriented organizations have an important set of questions to ask themselves and actions to undertake in order to create and nurture their spiritual existence. But once the trend is set, the sustenance should not be too hard to achieve.*

## Reflection Sheet

These areas represent the contents of this chapter that I consider applicable to my life:

These areas represent the contents of this chapter whose applicability to my life I question:

My personal opinions after reading this chapter:

What I would like to remember:

# Conclusion

This book provides the reader with an effective overview on how to institute and nurture spirituality in the workplace. At the same time, the book explains that workplace spirituality is not the same as religion—it is, rather, based on the spirit of cooperativeness, trust, and acceptance, which leads to higher return on investments and better organizational performance overall. We have demonstrated in this book that spiritually oriented organizations maintain better rapport with their stakeholders, starting with their workforce, and thereby remain capable of reinventing themselves in a fast-changing environment such as our current corporate world.

By focusing on all aspects of workplaces—employees, management, the organization as an entity, and ultimately, all other stakeholders—we attempted to provide an enhanced insight into the various levels that need to be examined when transforming an organization into a more spiritually attuned one.

The authors hope that this book has contributed toward the readers' understanding of the phenomenon of spirit in the workplace.

The authors cordially invite your feedback at the following email addresses:

Dr. Joan Marques: Jmarques01@earthlink.net
Dr. Satinder Dhiman: Satinder.Dhiman@Woodbury.edu
Dr. Richard King: Richking@att.net

# ᴇpilogue

In a recent workshop comprised of 75 percent baby boomers (born 1946-1964), 15 percent silent generation members (pre-1946), and 10 percent generation Xers (post-1964), a number of valuable issues surfaced. The focus of this meeting was spirituality in the workplace, and the authors of this book formed the panel of keynote speakers. The following summary provides some of the significant points that emerged interactively:

✓ Spirituality in the workplace consists of a set of closely interrelated themes such as morality, understanding, interconnectedness, respect, openness, honesty, trust, truth, giving, belief in a higher source, an aesthetically pleasing environment, team orientation, peace and harmony, acceptance, diversity, bonding, self motivation, and kindness.

✓ Spirituality is actually a natural process since it only requires a person to be his or her best, honest, and total self. However, it is not easy to practice and maintain in many workplaces because this natural behavior is not yet accepted in our highly individualistic society, in which we have been taught to only look out for ourselves.

✓ In a spiritual workplace the bottom line is not ignored, but rather enhanced in an alternative, excellent, effective way—by prioritizing fulfillment and quality of life through an interconnected approach. The spiritual leader knows that this is the preferred approach to achieve lasting excellence in organizational performance.

✓ A spiritual person is aware that harboring positive thoughts toward others will not only increase their well-being, but also deepen his or her own contentment. Likewise, such a person is also aware that harboring negative thoughts toward others not only diminishes their well-being, but also lessen his or her own contentment. In sum, spirituality makes one more responsible regarding one's feelings toward others and thereby enhances one's level of emotional intelligence.

✓ Spiritual people are driven by a desire to do well and to care. Although they may differ in their opinions regarding the source of this drive, whether it is God, the self, the soul, or nature, their agreement about the ultimate purpose of this drive outweighs all other differences.

163

✓ Spiritual people realize that they should learn from the past, plan for the future, but above all, value and live in the present. They know that the art of *being there*—the *power of now*(122)—provides its own rewards: lasting devotion from the ones they granted their undivided attention, enhanced earnings from the maximized performance they demonstrated, and a greater sense of inner peace for taking the time to "smell the roses."

✓ Spirituality is the breath that drives benign souls toward the achievement of a higher quality, not quantity, of life.

✓ The maturity process is one of the most powerful drivers in the emergence of a spiritual mindset (the very structure of the audience at this session was proof of this point: 90 percent were born before 1964). Interest in the spiritual dimension increases as life progresses and the end draws near. As the majority of today's executives reside in the baby boomer and silent generation age groups, it is understandable that the need for spirituality at work will only increase in the coming years.

✓ Spirituality at work will require concerted transformation in our individual thinking and societal performance. However, the call for its institution will not diminish, but rather surge on a global level as we move toward a greater interdependent world. This will ultimately lead to the change required for the emergence of spirituality in every direction.

> **The authors believe that the following sentence captures the essence of their book:**
> We are not *human beings* on a *spiritual journey.*
> We are *spiritual beings* on a *human journey.*

## Postscript for the Spiritual Worker

Eleven Reasons Why You Should Nurture A Spiritual Mindset

1.  All thoughts you harbor toward the environment have a reciprocal effect on you: harbor negative thoughts, and you will weaken yourself; harbor positive thoughts, and you will strengthen yourself.

2.  If you lend a helping hand or a listening ear, you will not only be intrinsically rewarded through a wonderful feeling of satisfaction for doing the right thing, but you will also receive extrinsic rewards by encountering gratitude in the most unexpected places and at the most unexpected times. "When you do the right thing, right things happen to you" (Jiddu Krishnamurti).

3.  Setbacks occur in everyone's life. The spiritual epiphany usually surfaces after confrontations with emotional, physical, financial, or mental hardship. Yet, why wait for the unavoidable wake up call if you are already awake?

4.  In retrospect, almost every memorable experience in your life is a non-materialistic one. This underscores the fact that you are a spiritual being having a human experience. Should you not, then, keep the awareness of the relativity of things in mind as a foundation for all your future decisions and acts?

5.  As diverse as the people in a workplace look, so diverse are their characters. The spiritual mind understands and respects that and works harmoniously with each individual—even the more difficult ones.

6.  Spirituality is an ever-elevating plane of caring, understanding, and respecting. A spiritual person is aware of the fact that he or she is still on his or her way to absolute spiritual performance, and is therefore appropriately humble. This humility enhances one's will to cooperate in fulfilling activities, and makes a spiritual worker a valuable one.

7.  A spiritual person is honest, open, and truthful, and, hence, free from having to remember any made-up stories or false attitudes. As they say, when you tell the truth you do not have to remember. Being spiritual therefore makes life less complicated.

8. Applying a spiritual approach at work will enhance an "at-home" feeling, which encourages creativity, proactivity, and responsibility among all members of the "family."

9. Spiritual people value each other's insights and therefore work very well in team settings: they are aware of the advantages of team building (recognition, enhanced involvement, networking, more in-depth output, and interconnectedness), and they contribute to the best of their capabilities. This leads to a higher level of organizational excellence.

10. Nurturing the spiritual mindset is just a matter of connecting with yourself without fear of what others may think of you. Spirituality, then, is nothing more or less than being your own best self. That should not be hard, should it?

> **Do all the good you can,**
> **In all the ways you can,**
> **With all the means you can,**
> **To all the people you can,**
> **As long as you can.**

# Appendix 1

# Interview Protocol

Questions:

1. **Definition of Spirituality in the Workplace**

    1.1. How would you describe spirituality in the workplace?

    1.2. What are some words that you consider to be crucial to a spiritual workplace?

    1.3. Do you consider these words applicable to all work environments that meet your personal standards of a spiritual workplace?

    1.4. What is essential for the experience of a spiritual workplace?

2. **Possible structural meanings of experiencing spirituality in the workplace**

    2.1. What does a spiritual worker do?

    2.2. What doesn't a spiritual worker do?

    2.3. What is difficult about being a spiritual worker?

    2.4. What is easy about being a spiritual worker?

3. **Underlying themes and contexts for the experience of a spiritual workplace**

    3.1. What will definitely be present in a spiritual workplace?

    3.2. What will definitely be absent in a spiritual workplace?

4. **General structures that precipitate feelings and thoughts about the experience of spirituality in the workplace**

    4.1. What are some of the *organizational* reasons that could influence the transformation from a non-spiritual workplace into a spiritual workplace?

4.2. From the *employee's perspective*, what are some of the reasons to transform from a non-spiritual to a spiritual employee?

## 5. Conclusion

Would you like to add, modify, or delete anything significant from the interview that would give a better or fuller understanding toward the establishment of a broadly acceptable definition of **"spirituality in the workplace"?**

*Thank you very much for your participation.*

# Appendix 2

# Horizonalization Table

# 2003 Interviews

| Questions: | Interviewee A | Interviewee B | Interviewee C | Interviewee D | Interviewee E | Interviewee F |
|---|---|---|---|---|---|---|
| **Demographics:** | | | | | | |
| • Gender | • Female | • Male | • Male | • Female | • Male | • Male |
| • Race | • Black | • Caucasian | • Caucasian | • Black | • Black | • Caucasian |
| • Age categ. | • 30-40yrs | • 50-60yrs | • 50-60yrs | • 50-60yrs | • 50-60yrs | • >70yrs |
| • Position | • Founder/CEO | • President | • Director | • Co-Founder/CEO | • Founder/CEO | • Founder/President |
| • Religion | • Christian | • Unknown | • Jewish | • General Religious | • General Religious | • Unknown |
| **R Q.1: Definition of spirituality in the workplace** | | | | | | |
| 1.1 How would you describe spirituality in the workplace? | • Being conscious that there is a higher power working on your behalf | • Karma: Individuals are guided by a higher source. It entails honesty, and doing unto others, as you want them to do to you. | • [Tying into] ethical behavior, appreciative behavior toward colleagues, clients<br>• It has to do with forms and attitudes of how you work with people, and the kind of climate that you set within the workplace. | • Relating to the power within, [...] becoming one with its wholeness, [and] expressing [it] in everything you do: with your employees, your projects, in your presence, [and] everything [else] you come in contact with | • The tone of the tenor in the work environment normally set by the person in charge<br>• All trying to do everything with God's help, knowing that if what we do is pleasing to him than we have his assistance<br>• People who are in | • Achieving a higher dimension of clarity and productivity, creativeness; operating at a dimension that is more concerned with the quality of life than the quantity of life<br>• It's of the spirit; it's the integration of the mind, body, emotions and the soul. |

| | |
|---|---|
| - It's not totally non-materialistic, because the process of spirituality can lead to material reward. | |
| alignment, comfortable, and willing to do the job | |
| | |
| - More productive<br>- A happier place to be<br>- A more effective organization for all<br>- [It has nothing to do with] traditional organized religion<br>- [An organization that is] focused on the way it serves the community and is part of the community | - More attention to cooperation versus a competition (a better balance between them) |
| | |
| | |

| | | | | | |
|---|---|---|---|---|---|
| **1.2** What are some words that you consider to be crucial to a spiritual workplace? | • Faith<br>• Confidence<br>• Belief<br>• Risk<br>• Strength | • Caring<br>• Understanding<br>• Team<br>• Achieving | • Cooperation<br>• Respect<br>• Appreciation (general)<br>• A natural energy (not imposed by upper management)<br>• Diversity (appreciating and understanding it)<br>• Perspective<br>• Ethics<br>• Trust | • Love<br>• Peace<br>• Joy<br>• Happiness<br>• God<br>• Harmony<br>• Perfection<br>• Understanding<br>• Truth<br>• Feeling<br>• Compassion | • God<br>• Calmness<br>• Respect<br>• No cursing<br>• Hope Faith<br>• Motivation<br>• Honesty | • Soul<br>• Heart<br>• Mind<br>• The integration of all of those<br>• Ethics<br>• Morality<br>• Commitment<br>• Perseverance - Those are all components of basic spirituality<br>• Honesty<br>• Straightforwardness |
| **1.3** Do you consider these words applicable to all work environments that meet your personal standards of a | Yes, because:<br>• Sometimes you may have to deal with people who are not easy to work with.<br>• Circumstances may not | Yes, because:<br>• You're still dealing with people no matter what the environment is. | Yes, because:<br>• they ought to apply everywhere. | Yes. | I think so.<br>• The leader always sets the tone, whether positive or negative. | Probably not.<br>• I think there are a few of those components that will foster spirituality in almost any circumstance. But I don't think you need all of those |

| Questions | Interviewee A | Interviewee B | Interviewee C | Interviewee D | Interviewee E | Interviewee F |
|---|---|---|---|---|---|---|
| spiritual workplace? | always fall into place.<br>• You always have to remain productive. | | | | | components to arrive at a spiritual base or spiritual motivation.<br>• You've got to pick and choose what components you're going to use (depending on the environment your workplace operates in). |
| 1.4 What is essential for the experience of a spiritual workplace? | • Surrounding: aesthetic/ sunlight/ a window<br>• It's appropriate to pray.<br>• Encouragement<br>• Having people of like minds | • Ability of the leader to convey his/her intent to employees | • Mutual respect<br>• Mutual appreciation<br>• A sense of purpose<br>• Intention to bring out the strengths of the people that comprise that workplace | • Centering one's self<br>• Meditation<br>• Reading<br>• Connecting with the power within | • That the person in charge be the main driver of that | • A receptivity to spirituality<br>• Responsiveness<br>• Sensitivity [...] to find the niche and the right buttons to press to move spirituality forward<br>• It has to start at the top.<br>• It starts as a personal thing. |

R Q. 2

| Possible structural meanings of experiencing spirituality in the workplace? | | | | | | |
|---|---|---|---|---|---|---|
| If a worker was operating at his or her highest level of spiritual awareness, what would he or she actually do? | • Be committed<br>• Caring to achieve completely and accurately<br>• Providing quality | • Seeking the truth<br>• Apply fairness<br>• Seeking to understand others | • Understand what the point of the work is<br>• [Understand] objectives and their value<br>• Looking to see how to make their contributions relevant and valuable for both the organization and him- or herself<br>• Self-motivated<br>• Work [...] hard<br>• Draw on the strengths of [...] colleagues<br>• Be more open | • Attract to him/herself all the information he/she needs in order to perform the task at hand<br>• Be able to get him- or herself out of the way (devoid of ego)<br>• Love doing what he/she is doing<br>• Not let time restrict the quality of his/her performance | • More driven to do a good job<br>• More motivated to do things right<br>• Be honest (have a hard time lying, even if it's for the sake of the boss or the company) | • Be a servant leader<br>• Be a giver<br>• Get fulfillment out of giving and helping others to get better in that organization<br>• Open up his or herself to new ideas from the organization<br>• Encourage other people to reduce the barriers that prevent those new things from coming in<br>• Be kind<br>• Will respect the environment<br>• Be a mentor |

| Questions: | Interviewee A | Interviewee B | Interviewee C | Interviewee D | Interviewee E | Interviewee F |
|---|---|---|---|---|---|---|
|  |  |  | • Expect:<br>  - Openness,<br>  - Sharing of information,<br>  - Good problem solving<br>• [Seeking ways to] make additional contribution, or improvements the organization would benefit from<br>• Understand [the place of his/her] contributions toward the success of the organization |  |  | • Be a good listener<br>• Be synthesizing<br>• Be motivating<br>• Encourage creativity<br>• Be direct<br>• Be honest<br>• Be straightforward |
| If a worker was operating at his or her highest level of spiritual awareness, what would he or she not do? | • Be negative<br>• Use bad language<br>• Be mean to people<br>• Have a messy | • Socialize too much<br>• Become a source of negativity | • Focus to get ahead at the expense of their peers<br>• [Be] primarily focused on their own needs | • Think of a task as "work" but rather as something he/she wants to do<br>• Be untruthful | • Lie<br>• Participate in any kind of dishonest activities be more<br>• Do anything displeasing to | • Be confrontational<br>• Be autocratic or authoritarian<br>• Be overly critical<br>• Punish people |

| | Interviewee A | Interviewee B | Interviewee C | Interviewee D | Interviewee E | Interviewee F |
|---|---|---|---|---|---|---|
| workplace | | | • Engage in any kind of backstabbing or withholding information [for power or competition purposes] <br> • Stop learning <br> • Assume he/she knows everything <br> • Shy away from making suggestions | • Be dishonest <br> • Mistrust | God <br> - Be malingering <br> - Be lazy | for mistakes, but rather see the value of mistakes and help others learn from them <br> • Be obsessed with organizational structure <br> • Be engaged in crass company politics |
| Questions: | | | • Hold on to one view so stubbornly that no progress could be made <br> • Provide obstacles to progress <br> • Refrain from speaking up <br> • Inappropriately divulge confidential | | | |

| | | | | | | |
|---|---|---|---|---|---|---|
| What is easy about living in alignment with spiritual values in the workplace? | • Being appreciative of what you have | • Having the spiritual mindset as a natural part of you instead of a learned one<br>• Open-mindedness<br>• Acceptance | • Trust [which will enable you to relax]<br>• Appreciation | • Everything...as long as you get yourself out of the way first | • It helps to make a more pleasant atmosphere<br>• People on the same level getting along better<br>• Be caring, loving, and supportive of others | • The personal fulfilment<br>• To live with yourself and be yourself without having multiple agenda's and having to worry about all that stuff |
| What is difficult about living in alignment with spiritual values in the workplace? | • Maintaining one's faith in difficult times | • Being harder on yourself<br>• Obtaining karma/Applying the golden rule | • Obtaining trust, as most workplaces that [..] don't generate and exhibit those qualities | • Erasing all the collective negative consciousness that you have collected over the years of living<br>- Filtering our consciousness [by distinguishing the spiritual impressions from information outside the information] | • It doesn't always lead to a pique of efficiency (the good worker can be taken advantage of by sly customers/colleagues) | • The difficult part is that the easy part is unnatural to the business organization - Business people are taught to focus on the quantity of life rather than the quality, so they suspect the one who comes with |

| | Interviewee A | Interviewee B | Interviewee C | Interviewee D | Interviewee E | Interviewee F |
|---|---|---|---|---|---|---|
| | • | • | • | the mere visual ones] <br> • | • | a different approach, telling them that it pays off even better! <br> So: the difficulty is: transferring who you really are into this massive organizational structure that has different priorities <br> **Interviewee F** <br> o **Not being ostracized by your peers in the organization** |
| **Questions:** | Interviewee A | Interviewee B | Interviewee C | Interviewee D | Interviewee E | Interviewee F |
| **R Q. 3** <br> Underlying themes and contexts for the experience of a spiritual workplace | | | | | | |
| 3.1 If an organization is consciously attempting to nurture | • An aesthetic environment (plants) <br> • Kind people <br> • Peace | • More group interaction <br> • More team goals <br> • More meetings | • Trust <br> • Respect <br> • Respect for differences <br> • Appreciation for what | • A beautiful atmosphere <br> • Soft music <br> • Books <br> • Plants <br> • Comfort | • Motivating faces <br> • Biblical material <br> • Motivational quotations | • at the top of the organization, you would see a group of top executives that would behave in a little |

| spirituality in the work-place, what will be present? | | | | | |
|---|---|---|---|---|---|
| | • More bonding of people<br>• Reflection of the spirit of intent that's placed in the workplace.<br>• Helping one another<br>• Sacrifices of personal goals to help others | • everyone brings to the table<br>• Involvement in important decisions<br>• Focus on what's working instead of only a focus on problems.<br>• A focus on how we work and what we do when we're most successful.<br>• Mentors<br>• A sense of mission that goes beyond the bottom line. | • Peace<br>• Pleasant smell<br>• Aura of joy and bliss<br>• Order | • A more conservative code of dress | • different manner: be more sensitive, kinder, smiling more: More aware of the humane factor, and that would be showing in their office structure; in their business demeanor: Kind of a caring environment<br>• Flexibility in accessing different levels of the organization<br>• Accessibility of information<br>• Casualness (lack of protocol)<br>• Conviviality among employees<br>• Clubs and organizational functions (fun things) |

| | Interviewee A | Interviewee B | Interviewee C | Interviewee D | Interviewee E | Interviewee F |
|---|---|---|---|---|---|---|
| | | | | | | • Fair compensation and good reward mechanisms<br>• Charity from the organization to the community |
| Questions: | • | • | • | • | • | Interviewee F<br>• A certain commonality in character<br>  - High ethical standards and moral standards<br>• More givers than takers |
| 3.2 If an organiza-tion is conscious-ly attempt-ing to nurture spirituality in the work-place, what will | • Poor aesthetics (loud music, anything that would not feed the spirit)<br>• Negative folks<br>• Lack of teamwork | • Long faces<br>• High stress level<br>• Absenteeism<br>• Tardiness<br>• Non-construc-tive arguing<br>• Lack of | • Mistrust<br>• Lack of appreciation<br>• Arbitrary decision making<br>• Tightly withheld or controlled information access | • Disorder<br>• Unhappy people<br>• Anger<br>• Tension<br>• Stress | • Offensive postings<br>• Offensive music<br>• Vulgar jokes | • A pressing drive to maximize profit and ROI<br>• Strong-willed, autocratic leaders<br>• Strong organizational structure<br>• Putting more emphasis on |

| | Interviewee A | Interviewee B | Interviewee C | Interviewee D | Interviewee E | Interviewee F |
|---|---|---|---|---|---|---|
| be absent | and effort | self-esteem | • Narrowly defined measures of success<br>• Punitive employee evaluations<br>• Objectives that are bordering on unethical…or …focused on loopholes<br>• Coercive leadership and invigorating fear | | | people as a resource over equipment and money |
| R Q. 4 General structures that precipitate feelings and thoughts about the experience of spirituality in the workplace. | | | | | | |
| Questions: | Interviewee A | Interviewee B | Interviewee C | Interviewee D | Interviewee E | Interviewee F |
| 4.1 What are some of the | • A difficult challenge | • The leadership | • Leader expectations | • Increased responsibility | • The leader's will to change: to | • That is totally experiential: Something has |

| | | | | | |
|---|---|---|---|---|---|
| *organizational* reasons that could influence the transformation from a workplace that does not consciously attempt to nurture spirituality and the human spirit to one that does? | • An unforeseen tragic event | | | | |
| | | | • The will to attract good people (workers and customers) to your business<br><br>• Loving leadership | enhance the quality of life in the work environment | to occur in the organization to make it happen<br>- Either an organizational experience, or a personal experience<br>- Personal: The CEO could be triggered by an experience to want to change the environment<br>- Organizational: The company can deteriorate in a certain regard (morale, productivity, efficiency), causing leaders to reconsider its rules of existence. |

| 4.1 From the employee's perspective, what are some of the reasons to transform from a worker who does not attempt to live and work with spiritual values and practices to one that does? | | | | | |
|---|---|---|---|---|---|
| • Surviving low points (tragedy) | • Handling job and personal stress<br>  - Desire to be healthier,<br>  - Desire to stop abusing drugs or other people)<br>• Obtaining positive influences from others<br>  - Desire for inner peace and self-satisfaction | • Reasoning (spiritual/intuitive, rather than rational)<br>  - Aversion of a competitive environment<br>    They will to feel better about one's self, work, colleagues, and society.<br>  - Aversion of a heavy-handed hierarchical structure<br>    The will to be involved in a successful, ground-breaking organization | • Openness to new ideas and a new way of thinking<br>• A raised level of consciousness | • Confrontation with a life-changing problem<br>• Change of habits (more spiritual)<br>• Change of lifestyle (getting married and starting to raise children—wanting to lead by example) | • A personal change (which can cause the employee to become spiritual WITHOUT working in a spiritual environment). But the change in that employee can lead to spiritual influence of the work environment.<br>• As a result of a company culture that's converted (if he/she wants to continue working and prospering in that spiritual organization) |

| Questions: | Interviewee A | Interviewee B | Interviewee C | Interviewee D | Interviewee E | Interviewee F |
|---|---|---|---|---|---|---|
| Interview Q. 5 Conclusion Would you like to add, modify or delete anything significant from the interview that would give a better or fuller understanding toward the establishment of a broadly acceptable definition of spirituality in the workplace | • It's a faith walk everyday<br>• The universe conspires to let you have the experience of success first [...] then you have to go through hard times [...] before you get to the ultimate place of success and while you're going through that experience, you really have to be open to allowing your faith | • Every person has a spirit<br>• Every group has a spirit<br>• Every leader should recognize that | • If you broaden the definition of what the workplace is to include, for example, the community, these same characteristics should hold.<br>- Functioning at a high level of spiritual awareness engenders trust and will be beneficial to the entire community.<br>- You will become a role model, not only within your immediate workplace, but also | • Spirituality and religion are two different things.<br>• Spirituality is the personal connection to that inner being that lets you know the I AM of who YOU ARE | • The teachings and practices of spirituality should start in schools.<br>• Change starts within a person and then broadens out to his/her environment.<br>• Change causes change. | • One thing that intrigues me is the connectivity factor<br>- I therefore think there should be the creation of an environment in an organization where people could particularly talk about it. That should be looked at and capitalized on.<br>• By using the process of spirituality and beginning to enhance creativity and innovativeness and taking people to |

| | | | |
|---|---|---|---|
| and spirituality to be nurtured, and to encourage others in your workplace<br><br>• You need to be mentally fit, and physically fit. And the spiritual part is of just as much impor-tance. | | between your organiza-tion and others outside. For every business is the product of a network | different levels, the end result of that can be far better returns than what we have today: Because we're multiplying productivity so much<br><br>• Despite the critics, the paradigm shift is happening, and it's going to take a while for business to really take the ball and run with it<br><br>• The issue that we're faced with in the world today—it has been proven—cannot be handled by governments; cannot be handled by non-profit organizations |

| Questions: | Interviewee A | Interviewee B | Interviewee C | Interviewee D | Interviewee E | Interviewee F |
|---|---|---|---|---|---|---|
| | | | | | | (NGO's). It's got to be handled a lot by the private sector. And that's the missing factor right now. |
| | | | | | | - Environmental issues, health care issues, care of the aging and security develop-ment, these are all what I call nurturing issues, and they can be handled best by the private sector, who can manage those issues |

# Appendix 3

# Horizonalization Table

# 2004 Questionnaire

| Question | Part.1 High School Affiliate | Part.2 Children's Foundation President | Part.3 Director of Education Music and Performing Arts Center | Part.4 Freelance Journalist and Art Advocate | Part.5 Real Estate broker and consultant. | Part.6 President ClearWater Technologies, Inc. | Part.7 Fund Development Consultant |
|---|---|---|---|---|---|---|---|
| Question 1: What, according to you, is the most widely applicable phrase for the trend described as the focus of this publication? | ? | In-depth view of personnel and their connections | Vision, "big ideas," the greater good, passion and purpose... This includes personal vision, intention, value, purpose and meaning in my daily life. This reflects who I am and what I do or what I contribute time, focus of energy, belief, expertise, passion, vision and sustained commitment to (and which may, for periods of time, be unacknowledged and unrewarded from external organizational structural and support systems). | Enhancing personal fulfillment and creativity through spirituality and enlightenment, both in and out of the workplace | Work as a life-fulfilling activity—not as a means to simply fund an otherwise personally fulfilling life | "An integrated life" | Seeing the potential for businesses to achieve enhanced goals by helping their people (at all levels) achieve personal fulfillment through their work |
| Question 2: In your opinion: what does this trend entail? | A focus on QUALITY and process | Looking deeper into the personal and spiritual connectedness in the particular organization and | Shifting the paradigm in all sectors of endeavor from "top-down" hierarchy to mentoring-trusting-sharing-teaming; from "simple bottom line | This trend entails, evaluating and seeking to understand ourselves both as individuals and in our interrelationships with others, by | Seeking an answer to the age old question of the meaning of our lives on this earth as we are caught up in a frenetically | 1. A sense of personal possibilities 2. A willing-ness to recognize another's | This trend entails sincerely and wisely embracing, nurturing and honoring the full potential of individuals (in the |

| | | | | | | |
|---|---|---|---|---|---|---|
| | personal goals | outcomes" to exploring complex problems and processes through group-determined enduring questions and guiding principles; seeking authentic connections among disciplines and areas of knowledge; a willingness to probe for deeper levels of truth and creative solutions; a tolerance for risk-taking and ambiguity | staring within and extending out to both the workplace and the world. To, as individuals, try to develop trust, and goodwill through honesty, kindness, love, and respect for others. | accelerating and increasingly complex post industrial world | 3. personal possibilities. A personal and work environment where this can occur; and is encouraged | organization), thereby engaging more fully their personal power to achieve their own as well as their organization's purposes. It entails looking at the whole system of an organization and the people who make it up. |
| Question 3: In your opinion: what does this trend NOT entail? | Not a focus on "The Bottom Line" | Regular ways of handling personnel, focus such as economic effects of world and local markets—downsizing, etc.—not reflective of problems that arise in this area | A "top-down" hierarchy "checklist" mentality" to simply manipulate situations to achieve profit and/or material outcomes without careful consideration of the impact on environmental, human and organic systems, short-term and long-term. Simplistic, lower-level thinking rather than complex problem solving and critical evaluative | It does not entail ruthless competition, cruelty, secrecy, dishonesty, greed, irresponsibility, backbiting, gossip, or slander, negativity, pitting one person against another, favoritism, and lastly, the need to win or achieve one's goal at any cost. | Quantifying success in terms of corporate or personal financial return or productivity of hours spent at work. Instead, use other measures of worker satisfaction such as the length of employment at the company, or whether employee's friends or relatives have been encouraged | Dishonest rewards, even those intended to encourage |
| | | | | | | This trend does not entail any wild-eyed adherence to an offbeat philosophy. |

| Question 4: How, according to you, can this trend be achieved? | | thinking | | | | | | |
|---|---|---|---|---|---|---|---|---|
| Admission that the prevailing focus in our culture, capitalism and free enterprise, which encourages materialism and competition, is destructive to human and other life on earth | Much insight—time spent with all concerned. National and Business school awareness that this new system works; trends take a long time to be realized | Change from within as well as with out or above. Commit to and learn to "let go" of controlling things in order to maintain status. Delegate, team, and collaborate. Employ reflective, creative, group-focused conversation and consensus building, decision making and processing tools and structures within the workplace in business and education (i.e., the old "military-industrial" education system is highly resistant to change). | to work at or do business with the company, or whether the job has stimulated social or charitable organizing by groups of workers within the workplace or outside the workplace. | Through leadership that sets an example of trust, honesty, and kindness, and expects the same from one's colleagues and employees. That the traits of firmness without cruelty are respected, as well as responsibility. That the rewards are generous in praise, advances in position and financial remuneration, but are earned. By increasing and encouraging teamwork, but always respectful of and open to the | Creating a "marriage" of employers and their employees by developing a means for employers and employees to devise and share common goals and means to achieve them | Honest opportunities, realistic challenges (including "impossible" ones that are acknowledged as such), appropriate rewards for success, support for efforts, meaningful criticism | Top leadership must carefully study the work experience of individuals in organizations. Leaders must be willing to examine the assumptions behind current practices, and develop/embrace new thinking where they find a need. They then must lead (and model) the changes necessary to unleash the power of each individual to contribute, while |

| Question 5: How, according to you, can this trend be sustained? | Wide-spread education to wake people up (consciousness); with tools to keep us awake | Agency and leadership must connect with staff and keep this concept going—through meetings and mentoring—offer some incentives for making good progress in the trend | - a critical mass of successful organizations and models that become visible, compelling and generative networking of like and diverse groups to demonstrate ability to align values, purpose and actions; model acceptance and accommodation of differences<br><br>- key funding and economic links to provide support and time for the | With every step of one's inner and outer spiritual growth, both the individuals and the groups involved should receive recognition, support, and praise. Sometimes this growth is a slow process, and encouragement should be generous. The rewards of a happier, more creative inner self and workplace will sustain the above. | individual's point of view, and rights to challenge any premise, no matter how different or unique these points of view may be | By constantly adding benefits (not necessarily monetary) to workers packages…not just what they buy into when they first accept employment. And, at the same time challenge workers to devise innovative services and benefits they can offer their employer or company. (e.g., marketing their company by co-branding themselves with | If the above are functional, they should be self-sustaining | enhancing her loyalty and commitment to the work of the organization. At the same time they will be assisting individuals to achieve their own personal fulfillment.<br><br>This trend can be sustained once the approach is understood to be at least as productive as those systems that are based primarily on the "dollar bottom-line." Businesses then will be more willing to add "quality of life" dimensions to their goals and purposes. |

| | | | |
|---|---|---|---|
| paradigm shifts and documentation of impact - time to realize what is being learned and to practice doing things differently | | their company in their outside social and charitable activities) | |

# Notes

1. Brandt, E. (1996). Corporate pioneers explore spirituality. *HR Magazine, 41*, 82.
2. Rosner, B. (2001). Is there room for the soul at work? *Workforce, 80*(2), 82-83.
3. Ashmos, D., P., & Duchon, D. (2000). Spirituality at work: A conceptualization and measure. *Journal of Management Inquiry, 9*(2), 137.
4. Laabs, J. (1995). Balancing spirituality and work. *Personnel Journal, 74*(9), 60.
5. Thompson, W. (2001). Spirituality at work. *Executive Excellence, 18*(9), 10.
6. Ashmos, D., P., & Duchon, D. (2000). Spirituality at work: A conceptualization and measure. *Journal of Management Inquiry, 9*(2), 137.
7. Laabs, J. (1995). Balancing spirituality and work. *Personnel Journal, 74*(9), 60.
8. Schrage, M. (2000, October 5). Sorry about the profit, boss. My feng shui is off. *Fortune, 142*, 306.
9. Oldenburg, D., & Bandsuch, M. (1997, May 7). The spirit at work: Companies should nurture the soul if they want more from employees. *The Detroit News.*
10. Goforth, C. (2001, October 7). Spirituality enters the office: A growing number of business executives are acting on the conviction that faith has a purpose in the workplace. *The Ottawa Citizen*, K2.
11. Kahnweiler, W., & Otte, F. (1997). In search of the soul of HRD. *Human Resource Development Quarterly, 8*(2), 171.
12. Ashmos, D., P., & Duchon, D. (2000). Spirituality at work: A conceptualization and measure. *Journal of Management Inquiry, 9*(2), 134-145.
13. Stewart, C. S. (2002). Soul time. *Potentials, 35*(9), 92.
14. Bolman, L., & Deal, T. (1999). *Reframing organizations: Artistry, choice, and leadership.* San Francisco: Jossey-Bass.
15. Cash, K., Gray, G., & Rood, S. (2000). A framework for accommodating religion and spirituality in the workplace/Executive commentary. *The Academy of Management Executive, 14*(3), 124-134.
16. Cavanagh, G. (1999). Spirituality for managers: Context and critique. *Journal of Organizational Change Management, 12*(3), 186.
17. Cavanagh, G. (1999). Spirituality for managers: Context and critique. *Journal of Organizational Change Management, 12*(3), 186.
18. Bruce, W. M. (2000). Public administrator attitudes about spirituality: An exploratory study. *American Review of Public Administration, 30*(4), 460-472.
19. Mitroff, I., & Denton, E. (1999). *A spiritual audit of corporate America: A hard look at spirituality, religion, and values in the workplace.* San Francisco: Jossey-Bass.
20. Adler, M. J. (1992). *Truth in religion: Plurality of religions and unity of truth.* New York: Collier Books.
21. Freshman, B. (1999). An exploratory analysis of definitions and applications of spirituality in the workplace. *Journal of Organizational Change Management, 12*(4), 318.
22. Laabs, J. (1995). Balancing spirituality and work. *Personnel Journal, 74*(9), 60.

23. Giacalone, R. A., & Jurkiewicz, C. L. (2004). A values framework for measuring the impact of workplace spirituality on organizational performance. *Journal of Business Ethics, 49*(2), 129.
24. Stewart, C. S. (2002). Soul time. *Potentials, 35*(9), 92.
25. Ashmos, D., P., & Duchon, D. (2000). Spirituality at work: A conceptualization and measure. *Journal of Management Inquiry, 9*(2), 134-145.
26. Robin, R. (2003). Healthy, wealthy and wise: More companies are realizing that wellness programs make very good business sense. *Canadian Business, 76*(23).
27. Gull, G. A., & Doh, J. (2004). The "transmutation" of the organization: Toward a more spiritual workplace. *Journal of Management Inquiry, 13*(2), 128.
28. Mohamed, A. A., Wisnieski, J., Askar, M., & Syed, I. (2004). Toward a theory of spirituality in the workplace. *Competitiveness Review, 14*(1/2), 102.
29. Giacalone, R. A., & Jurkiewicz, C. L. (2003). Right from wrong: The influence of spirituality on perceptions of unethical business activities. *Journal of Business Ethics, 46*(1), 85.
30. Giacalone, R. A., & Jurkiewicz, C. L. (2003). Right from wrong: The influence of spirituality on perceptions of unethical business activities. *Journal of Business Ethics, 46*(1), 85.
31. Carter, D. (2003). Editorial. *Training Journal*, 1.
32. Sangster, C. (2003). Spirituality in the workplace: Finding the holistic happy medium. *Training Journal*, 16.
33. Gull, G. A., & Doh, J. (2004). The "transmutation" of the organization: Toward a more spiritual workplace. *Journal of Management Inquiry, 13*(2), 128.
34. Johnson, H. (2004). Taboo no more. *Training, 41*(4), 22.
35. Ashar, H., & Lane-Maher, M. (2004). Success and spirituality in the new business paradigm. *Journal of Management Inquiry, 13*(3), 249.
36. Garcia-Zamor, J.-C. (2003). Workplace spirituality and organizational performance. *Public Administration Review, 63*(3).
37. Turner, J. (1999). Spirituality in the workplace. *CA Magazine, 132*(10), 41.
38. Wheatley, M. (2002). Spiritual leadership. *Executive Excellence, 19*(9), 6.
39. Mitroff, I., & Denton, E. (1999). *A spiritual audit of corporate America: A hard look at spirituality, religion, and values in the workplace.* San Francisco: Jossey-Bass, 23-25.
40. DeCenzo, D., & Robbins, S. (1998). *Human resource management* (6th ed.). New York: John Wiley & Sons, 9.
41. DeCenzo, D., & Robbins, S. (1998). *Human resource management* (6th ed.). New York: John Wiley & Sons, 38.
42. DeCenzo, D., & Robbins, S. (1998). *Human resource management* (6th ed.). New York: John Wiley & Sons, 33.
43. DeCenzo, D., & Robbins, S. (1998). *Human resource management* (6th ed.). New York: John Wiley & Sons, 33.
44. Verespej, M. (2001, June 11). How to solve the worker shortage [Internet, LexisNexis Academic Universe-Document]. *Industry Week*, 23 (2001, September 23).
45. Gilbert, J. (2000). An empirical examination of resources in a diverse environment [Internet, proquest.umi.com]. *International Personnel Management Association Summer 2000*, (2), 175 (2001, September 8).

46. Centaur Communications Ltd., 2001, S03.
47. Alger, J. (1997). The educational value of diversity [Internet]. *American Association of University Professors,* ¶4. URL *http://www.aaup.org/ aadivart.htm* (2001, September 23).
48. Thomas, C. (2001). Challenges to diversity: Recruiting and retaining minorities. *Pharmaceutical Executive,* 10-15.
49. Richard, O. C., & Johnson, N. B. (2001). Understanding the impact of human resource diversity practices on firm performance [Internet, Proquest.umi.com]. *Journal of Managerial Issues,* 180-190 (2001, September 8).
50. Centaur Communications Ltd., 2001, S03.
51. Richard, O. C., & Johnson, N. B. (2001). Understanding the impact of human resource diversity practices on firm performance [Internet, Proquest.umi.com]. *Journal of Managerial Issues,* 192 (2001, September 8).
52. Grensing-Pophal, L. (2000). Is your HR department diverse enough? [Internet, Proquest.umi.com]. *HR Magazine,* 46-47 (2001, September 8).
53. Richard, O. C., & Johnson, N. B. (2001). Understanding the impact of human resource diversity practices on firm performance [Internet, Proquest.umi.com]. *Journal of Managerial Issues,* 178 (2001, September 8).
54. Grensing-Pophal, L. (2000). Is your HR department diverse enough? [Internet, Proquest.umi.com]. *HR Magazine,* 46 (2001, September 8).
55. Richard, O. C., & Johnson, N. B. (2001). Understanding the impact of human resource diversity practices on firm performance [Internet, Proquest.umi.com]. *Journal of Managerial Issues,* 192 (2001, September 8).
56. Rosner, B. (2001). Is there room for the soul at work? *Workforce, 80*(2), 82-83.
57. Paterson, A. (2000, 23 May). *Religion versus spirituality* [Internet]. URL *http://www.vision.net.au/~apaterson/esoteric/religion_spirituality.htm* (2002, January, 23).
58. Hamel, G. (2000). *Leading the revolution.* Boston: Harvard Business School Press, 209.
59. Hamel, G. (2000). *Leading the revolution.* Boston: Harvard Business School Press, 209.
60. Schein, E. (1984). Coming to a new awareness of organizational culture. *Sloan Management Review, 25*(000002), 3.
61. Kinicki, A., & Williams, B. (2003). *Management.* New York: John E. Biernat, 246.
62. Kinicki, A., & Williams, B. (2003). *Management.* New York: John E. Biernat, 246.
63. Schermerhorn, J. (2002). *Management* (7th ed.). New York: John Wiley & Sons, 49.
64. Kinicki, A., & Williams, B. (2003). *Management.* New York: John E. Biernat, 523.
65. Wolf, E. J. (2004). Spiritual leadership: A new model. *Healthcare Executive, 19*(2), 26.
66. Giacalone, R. A., & Jurkiewicz, C. L. (2004). A values framework for measuring the impact of workplace spirituality on organizational performance. *Journal of Business Ethics, 49*(2), 129.

67. Garcia-Zamor, J.-C. (2003). Workplace spirituality and organizational performance. *Public Administration Review, 63*(3), 355.
68. Giacalone, R. A., & Jurkiewicz, C. L. (2004). A Values Framework for Measuring the Impact of Workplace Spirituality on Organizational Performance. *Journal of Business Ethics, 49*(2).
69. Collins & Porras, 1997; Pfeffer, 1988; Levey & Levey, 2000.
70. Garcia-Zamor, J.-C. (2003). Workplace spirituality and organizational performance. *Public Administration Review, 63*(3).
71. Raelin, J. (2004). The "bottom line" of leaderful practice (January/February 2004, ¶13), [Internet]. Ivey Management Services. URL *http://www.iveybusinessjournal.com/view_article.asp?intArticle_ID=462* (2004, October 29).
72. McLaughlin, C. (1998). Spirituality at work. *The Bridging Tree, 2004*(October 29), 11.
73. Guillory, W. (2002). Spirituality can be key to business success, Guillory tells Catholic Charities meeting [Internet]. *The Catholic Health Association of the United States.* URL *http://www.chausa.org/CELEB275/020803A.ASP* (2004, October 29).
74. Clark, E. (2001, August 8). Spirituality goes to work [Internet]. *BBC News Online*, ¶29. URL *http://news.bbc.co.uk/1/hi/business/1475995.stm (2004,* March 17).
75. Milliman, J., Ferguson, J., Trickett, D., & Condemi, B. (1999). Spirit and community at Southwest Airlines: An investigation of a spiritual values-based model. *Journal of Organizational Change Management, 12*(3), 221.
76. Freiberg, K. & Frieberg, J. (1996). *Nuts! Southwest Airlines' crazy recipe for business and personal success.* Austin: Bard Books.
77. Chappell, T. (1993). *The soul of a business.* New York: Bantam Books.
78. Chappell, T. (1999). *Managing upside down: The seven intentions of values-centered leadership.* New York: William Morrow.
79. Cavanagh, G., & Bandsuch, M. (2002). Virtue as a benchmark for spirituality in business. *Journal of Business Ethics, 38*(1/2), 109-118.
80. Chambers, N. (1998). The really long view. *Management Review, 87*(1), 10-16.
81. Korac-Kakabadse, N., Kouzmin, A., & Kakabadse, A. (2002). Spirituality and leadership praxis. *Journal of Managerial Psychology, 17*(3), 165.
82. Cavanagh, G. (1999). Spirituality for managers: context and critique. *Journal of Organizational Change Management, 12*(3), 186.
83. Anonymous. (1997). DePree receives business enterprise lifetime achievement award. *Facilities Design & Management, 16*(4), 10.
84. Koudal, P., & Lavieri, T. (2003). Profits in the balance. *Optimize*, 81.
85. Epictetus [Internet]. URL *http://quotations.about.com/cs/inspiration quotes/a/Attitude16.htm* (2004, October 24).
86. Victor Frankl. Attitude quotes [Internet]. URL http://quotations.about.com/cs/inspirationquotes/a/Attitude3.htm (2004, October 25).
87. Unknown. Attitude quotes [Internet]. URL *http://quotations.about.com/cs/inspirationquotes/a/Attitude3.htm* (2004, October 25).
88. Brandt, E. (1996). Corporate pioneers explore spirituality. *HR Magazine, 41*, 82.
89. Mitroff, I., & Denton, E. (1999). *A spiritual audit of corporate America: A hard look at spirituality, religion, and values in the workplace.* San Francisco: Jossey-Bass.

90. Chappel, T. (1993). *The soul of a business.* New York: Bantam Books; Interviewee F.
91. Interviewees A, D, E, and F.
92. Interviewees C and F.
93. Schermerhorn, J. (2002). *Management* (7th ed.). New York: John Wiley & Sons.
94. Kinicki, A., & Williams, B. (2003). *Management.* New York: John E. Biernat, 283
95. Weston, S. (2002). Faith at work. *New Zealand Management, 49*(3), 28.
96. Anonymous. (2003). Motivation secrets of the 100 best employers. *HR Focus, 80*(10), 1.
97. Kulesa, P. (2003). Keeping the good apples. *Security Management, 47*(8), 32.
98. Weston, S. (2002). Faith at work. *New Zealand Management, 49*(3), 28.
99. Caudron, S. (2001). Meditation and mindfulness at Sounds True. *Workforce, 80*(6), 40.
100. Hughes, R., Ginnett, R., & Curphy, G. (2002). *Leadership: Enhancing the lessons of experience.* New York: John E. Biernat.
101. Anonymous. (2001). HR specialists "will lead e-business." *Human Resource Management International Digest, 9*(1), 29.
102. Chalofsky, N. (2003). Meaningful work. *T+D, 57*(12), 52.
103. Marques, J. (2004). What motivation, satisfaction, and performance have to do with each other [Internet]. URL http://www.hillsorient.com/articles/2004/03/016.html (2004, March 21).
104. Marques, J. (2004). What motivation, satisfaction, and performance have to do with each other [Internet]. URL http://www.hillsorient.com/articles/2004/03/016.html (2004, March 21).
105. Hughes, R., Ginnett, R., & Curphy, G. (2002). *Leadership: Enhancing the lessons of experience.* New Yrk: John E. Biernat.
106. Caudron, S. (2001). Meditation and mindfulness at Sounds True. *Workforce, 80*(6), 40.
107. Anonymous. (2001). HR specialists "will lead e-business." *Human Resource Management International Digest, 9*(1), 29.
108. Chappell, T. (1993). *The soul of a business.* New York: Bantam Books.
109. DeCenzo, D., & Robbins, S. (1998). *Human resource management* (6th ed.). New York: John Wiley & Sons, 100.
110. Dorsey, D. (1998). The new spirit of work. *Fast Company,* (16), 224-232.
111. DeCenzo, D., & Robbins, S. (1998). *Human resource management* (6th ed.). New York: John Wiley & Sons, 104.
112. Green, T. (2000). Three steps to motivating employees. *HR Magazine, 45*(11), 155-158.
113. DeCenzo, D., & Robbins, S. (1998). *Human resource management* (6th ed.). New York: John Wiley & Sons, 111-118.
114. McDonald, M. (1999). Shush. The guy in the cubicle is meditating. *Business & Technology* (May 3, 1999).
115. Cash, K., Gray, G., & Rood, S. (2000). A framework for accommodating religion and spirituality in the workplace/Executive commentary. *The Academy of Management Executive, 14*(3), 124-134.
116. Caudron, S. (2001). Meditation and mindfulness at Sounds True. *Workforce, 80*(6), 45.

117. Laabs, J. (1995). Balancing spirituality and work. *Personnel Journal, 74*(9), 63-65.
118. Laabs, J. (1995). Balancing spirituality and work. *Personnel Journal, 74*(9), 165-166.
119. Rosner, B. (2001). Is there room for the soul at work? *Workforce, 80*(2), 82-83.
120. Anonymous. (2001). HR specialists "will lead e-business." Human Resource Management International Digest, 9(1), 29.
121. Anonymous. (2001). HR specialists "will lead e-business." Human Resource Management International Digest, 9(1), 29.
122. Tolle, E. The power of now: A guide to spiritual enlightenment. Vancouver: Namaste Publishing, 1997.

# Index

# About the Authors

**Dr. Joan Marques** worked for more than 20 years in advertising; radio and television hosting and production; and dynamic entrepreneurship. She founded and managed a business and a non-profit organization before emigrating from Suriname, South America, to the United States (Burbank, California). She holds a B.Sc. in Business Economics from MOC (Suriname), an MBA from Woodbury University, and a Doctorate in Organizational Leadership from Pepperdine University. She has done significant research on the topics of spirituality in the workplace and awakened leadership, and has authored a wide variety of articles as well as two books pertaining to workplace contentment and emotional intelligence for audiences in different continents of the globe.

**Dr. Satinder Dhiman** has guided business leaders for the last 28 years and served for 10 years as a Senior Lecturer in Commerce at DAV College in North India. He has co-authored various textbooks in the area of accounting and management. He currently serves ⁄as Professor of Management and as Associate Dean of Business at Woodbury University. Dr. Dhiman won ACBSP's prestigious International Teaching Excellence Award in 2004 and the Steve Allen "Excellence in Education" Award in 2006. He holds a Masters degree in Commerce (with Gold Medal) from Panjab University, India; a Doctorate in Organizational Leadership from Pepperdine University; and has completed Executive Leadership Programs at Stanford and Harvard. His current research interests include transformational leadership and spirituality in the workplace.

**Dr Richard King** is a recognized authority on United States⹁ Pacific Rim business relations, and founded his company, King International Group, to carry out his personal commitment to strengthening these relations. He has held top management positions at major organizations and currently serves on the boards of various Pacific Rim-oriented organizations. He is a longtime member of the Noetic Institute and the World Business Academy. Dr. King is a frequent writer and speaker on Pacific Rim business issues, and is the initiator of the *Business Renaissance* consulting project, which focuses on adding humanity to the bottom line. He holds a B. Sc. from Syracuse University, an M.A. from Occidental College, and an Honorary Doctorate of Business Administration from Woodbury University.